Voices

The Comanche Raid of 1776
& Other Tales of New Mexico History

by Robert J. Tórrez

Published by Rio Grande Books
Los Ranchos, New Mexico

Rio Grande Books
Los Ranchos, New Mexico
www.RioGrandeBooks.com

Printed in the U.S.A.
Book design by Paul Rhetts

Library of Congress Cataloging-in-Publication Data

Names: Tórrez, Robert J., author.
Title: Voices from the past : the Comanche Raid of 1776 and other true stories of New Mexico history / Robert J. Tórrez.
Other titles: Comanche Raid of 1776 and other true stories of New Mexico history
Description: Los Ranchos, New Mexico : Rio Grande Books, [2017]
Identifiers: LCCN 2017008417 | ISBN 9781943681181 (pbk. : alk. paper)
Subjects: LCSH: New Mexico--History. | New Mexico--Biography. | Frontier and pioneer life--New Mexico--Anecdotes. | Outlaws--New Mexico--History--Anecdotes.
Classification: LCC F796 .T67 2017 | DDC 978.9--dc23
LC record available at https://lccn.loc.gov/2017008417

Cover: Illustration by Jazz Tórrez

Contents

Introduction

The true stories and articles in this volume are based on "Voices From the Past," a monthly column I have been writing since 1992. Late that year, Amy Manning contacted me about writing a regular column about New Mexico history for *Santa Fe Pride*, a bi-monthly newspaper she was publishing. She characterized the newspaper as a publication that would emphasize "good news," positive stories about the people, places, and events of Santa Fe and the surrounding area. She felt that a column about New Mexico history and its historic figures would be a great addition to the paper's appeal. At that time, I had served as the New Mexico State Historian for little over five years but I had been doing research at the state archives since 1971, so when Amy contacted me about contributing a column to her newspaper, I did not have to think twice about it; I knew immediately this was the opportunity I had sought for some time; an opportunity that fit my own mandate as State Historian – to enhance the public's knowledge of and appreciation for New Mexico's history and cultural resources. As state historian I had the great privilege of working daily among the extraordinary and often underutilized resource we have in our own Spanish, Mexican, and Territorial - era archives, truly one of New Mexico's most valuable cultural treasures. As I spoke to Amy that day, I already had topics in mind for a number of story lines - as well as a title for the column - "Voices From the Past."

When I began my own research at the state archives more than four decades ago, it did not take long for me to realize that thousands of untold stories lurked in the tens of thousands of documents that filled the shelves of the archives vault. When I was appointed state historian in 1987, the vault consisted of a sliding door that led to the vast basement of the old Ilfeld warehouse on the corner of Montezuma Avenue and Guadalupe Street where the state records center and archives was located. Staff that had worked there since the facility opened in the early 1960s may have even hinted they often heard strange noises, the creaking and settling of an old building, no doubt, but it was an ambience that planted in one's mind the possibility that the place may have been haunted. I like to think that if there were strange noises heard in that old building, they emanated from the countless pages of letters, reports, and ledgers that crowded the shelves of that basement – both ancient and much more recent voices from the past, all straining to be heard.

That crowded, somewhat musty, and totally inadequate environment underwent a significant change in 1998. That year a long-awaited move from the old archives building on Montezuma was accomplished when the archives were transferred to the new, state-of- the- art building on Camino Carlos Rey that also houses the New Mexico State Library. Now, instead of the clanking of a sliding door, held closed by a chain and padlock, the click of an electronically activated lock invites entry into a clean, well-lit, modern, and safe storage facility. Except that when the door is swung open, there is a sort of whistle or "whoosh," a rush of air, caused, I am told, by the difference in air pressure between the entrance hall and the dedicated HVAC system of the vault where the archives are kept. To me, however, it sounds like a haunting voice that beckons us to enter and discover therein an endless variety of stories of little-known aspects of our history and the people that lived it.

That was the genesis of "Voices From the Past" as the column appeared regularly in *Santa Fe Pride* from November 1992 until February 1996, when the paper ceased publication. Soon afterward, Girard and Janet Iff, publishers of *Round the Roundhouse,* asked me to continue the monthly articles for their own newspaper and the first "Voices From the Past" column appeared in this new venue in the August 29, 1996 issue. The column has since developed into one of the paper's more popular features and has achieved a number of milestones. The one - hundredth column in 2002; number two hundred little less than a decade later in 2010; and now, as we approach a quarter century of publication, the count of monthly "Voices From the Past" columns continues onward to three hundred, with *Round the Roundhouse* under the new ownership of the late John Hetzler and wife Carol.

Another milestone for "Voices From the Past" was reached in 2004, when the University of New Mexico Press published a compilation of thirty-seven columns under the title *UFOs Over Galisteo and Other Stories of New Mexico History.* The book consists of a selection from the more than one hundred columns that had been published under the byline between 1992 and 2004. In retrospect, the title is deceptive. It gives the impression the book is about UFOs and I have often had to explain that the title comes from only one of the stories, which is based on a *Santa Fe New Mexican* report that appeared under the headline, "A Mysterious Aerial Phantom." The article concerned the reported sighting of what may have been a hot-air balloon south of Santa Fe in 1880! The sighting may have also been the hallucinations of overdone celebration but if anything was seen flying in the skies at that time, it would have certainly been more mysterious than any contemporary sighting, decades before anything happened near Roswell. Amazingly, since the original column on the UFO sighting was published in 1996, readers have informed me that the Galisteo Basin has a history of mysterious sightings and several have suggested that ancient petroglyphs found among the lava outcroppings in the area look like flying saucers!

Several columns that have appeared in the pages of *Santa Fe Pride* and *Round the Roundhouse* have subsequently provided the basis for full- fledged research projects that evolved into chapter-length stories in subsequent publications. Some columns about crime and punishment in territorial New Mexico, such as the "The Man Who was Hanged Twice," and stories about Paula Angel, Alma Lyons and Valentina Madrid, some of the most notorious females in New Mexico history, evolved into full chapters in my book, *Myth of the Hanging Tree* (University of New Mexico Press, 2008).

In one of the first articles I wrote for *Santa Fe Pride* in 1992, I used the words of Gaspar Pérez de Villagrá, author of *Historia de la Nueva México* that was published in 1610. "Through history those men are heroes whose deeds have been given proper recognition by the historian's pen," wrote Villagrá. "Others whose lives are unrecorded, did nothing, for of these our annals are silent and we know them not." Villagrá's words remind us that most of history consists of the lives and actions of those who seldom appear in the pages of our history books. The goal of these monthly "Voices From the Past" columns has been to bring to light the stories of some of those people whose voices have been forgotten or never heard by history.

As I look over the titles that have been published during the nearly quarter century since the first column appeared in *Santa Fe Pride*, I marvel at the diversity of topics the series has covered. Some of the "Voices From the Past" columns of which I am most proud are the short biographies of the important and famous as well as some relatively unknown figures in New Mexico history. The stories of individuals that were featured in early columns and published in the UFOs volume, such as presidio soldier Antonio Sena, J. Francisco Chaves, New Mexico's first official historian, the memoirs of Ena Marcil growing up in the mining town of Good Hope (Hopewell) in the 1880s, frontier scout Tomás Chacón and pesky Andrew P. Morris, come readily to mind.

This volume continues that theme of telling about the lives of people. "Letters from the Front" looks at two letters written by New Mexico Mounted Volunteers Carpio and José Dolores Silva to their family from an isolated northern New Mexico military outpost in 1866 and 1867. Others tell of the small pox epidemic of 1780 and the subsequent introduction of smallpox vaccination to New Mexico in 1805 by the military surgeon Cristobal Larrañaga, as well as the poignant and heart-felt speech Juan Bautista Vigil y Alarid delivered on the Santa Fe plaza when General Steven Watts Kearny occupied the capitol in August 1846. We also learn about outlaws Nicolás Aragón, José D. Gallegos, and gangster John Looney, whose story was prompted by my own grandmother's yarns about a "Chicago gangster" she knew; and of special note, wily Ada Humes, whose antics earned her the notoriety of a newspaper headline that labeled her "A Murderess in Clover," and about whom a long-time colleague, Susan Berry, is currently working on a book-length manuscript. And of course, it was necessary to include some of the "good guys," such as frontier judge Elisha V. Long, New Mexico State University horticulturalist Fabian García, and Governor George Curry.

This volume is presented in three parts. The first is a series of columns that tell of places, people and events during the Spanish (1598-1821) and Mexican (1821-1846) eras of New Mexico history. These stories range from the mundane, such as the formal contract for a horse race held in 1846 (the results of which remain unknown); the building of a bridge over the Rio Grande and the regulations for branding livestock, to the serious business of the orderly succession of the office of governor during the Mexican era and the unknown fate of six Apache captives in the early eighteenth century.

The sources utilized for these stories from this era are almost exclusively from New Mexico's Spanish and Mexican- era archival collections held at the New Mexico State Records Center and Archives in Santa Fe. The microfilm versions of these collections are found in the *Calendar to the Microfilm Edition of the Land Records of New Mexico, Series I, Calendar of the Microfilm Edition of the Spanish Archives of New Mexico, 1621 – 1821,* and the *Calendar of the Microfilm Edition of the Mexican Archives of New Mexico, 1821-1846.* The individual stories are not footnoted but each one contains enough information that readers who might be interested in checking the original sources or expanding on these short stories should have little trouble finding them.

Part two extends the theme of people, places and events into our Territorial period (1846-1912), although a few expand that time line beyond 1912, into early statehood. The materials for most of these stories come from the *Calendar to the Microfilm Edition of the Territorial Archives of New Mexico* although a significant portion is taken from newspapers of the period and some, such as the letters of Judge Elisha V. Long, and those of Carpio and José Dolores Silva, which are not microfilmed, are found in the private collection category at the state archives in Santa Fe.

Part three covers a wide variety of stories about the men and women we learn about because they got into trouble with the law. These stories are taken from a broad variety of sources found at the state archives, including the extensive penal papers found in the records of New Mexico's territorial-era governors, the district courts, and reports of crime and punishment found in period newspapers. It is great fun to come across a newspaper story on a crime, be it a robbery or murder, and then find an associated record of indictment, trail, and sentence (as well as acquittals) in the archives' district court records, and subsequently, as in the1893 case of José D. Gallegos, the subject of the Penitentiary of New Mexico's first "mug shot," records of incarceration in the territorial penitentiary.

The research and writing of this column has been one of the most enjoyable aspects of my professional life. It seems that almost every document I look at provides the basis for a story, fulfilling that part of the word "history" that makes the past so interesting. Luckily for us, the records in our state archives span the centuries of New Mexico's long and fascinating history and will surely provide sources for countless more stories that remain to be told. To paraphrase a common refrain, "so many stories, so little time."

I have heard writers say they write because something compels them to do so. It is possible my writing is thus motivated, but the reality is that I do not consider myself a writer. I rather describe myself as a fuddy-duddy historian who happens to write a lot. I do not write fiction, partly because I don't feel I have the admirable talent or imagination that genre requires, but mostly because I consider the truth to often be much more interesting than anything the most vivid imagination can conjure. I long ago decided to let the documents speak for themselves and let the often unfinished or incomplete stories that unfold therein have their say about New Mexico's history. As I noted in the short piece I contributed to *Voices of New Mexico*, published by Rio Grande Books in 2011 as a New Mexico Book Co-op project of New Mexico's Statehood Centennial, there are so many voices from the past that cry out to be heard. For better or for worse, "I too lived here and contributed to what we are today," they seem to say; and I hear the voices and write so that they might not be forgotten. The fifty-five columns in this volume are but a small sample of those stories that we hope will not only entertain, but enhance the reader's knowledge and appreciation of New Mexico's extraordinary past.

Robert J. Tórrez

Part One: Spanish and Mexican-era New Mexico

Registration of Livestock Brands

Livestock played an important role in the life and economy of colonial New Mexico. Sheep provided meat, wool, and a currency of exchange for trade with northern Mexico. Cattle, although not as important as sheep, provided meat and hides. Horses, mules, oxen and burros also had their role in transportation of people and goods. The importance of horse and mules is often reflected in litigation over ownership of individual animals that often took years to resolve.

To combat the ongoing problems caused by disputes over ownership of livestock, the Spanish and Mexican governments regularly issued orders and regulations that required livestock owners to register their brands and local officials to maintain a permanent record of these registrations. One of the earliest brand registrations found in New Mexico's Spanish Archives belonged to Diego Marques of Santa Cruz de la Cañada. On October 24, 1716, Marques, who described himself as a native of New Mexico, applied to Juan García de la Rivas, *alcalde mayor* (principal alcalde) of the Cañada jurisdiction, for approval of a brand. Marques noted the brand he was submitting was the same brand that had been previously approved for his father by Spanish authorities, possibly prior to the Pueblo Revolt of 1680 or shortly after the re-conquest in 1692 -93. Rivas certified the brand and deposited a copy of the registration in the archives of the local *cabildo*, from where the document found its way into the Spanish Archives of New Mexico, where it remains to this day.

Diego Marquez brand, 1714. Spanish Archives of New Mexico 1621-1846. #275.

Another early registered brand belongs to Francisco Valdes y Bustos, also of northern New Mexico. On November 8, 1752, Valdes y Bustos, a *vecino* (Spanish citizen) of Santa Cruz de la Cañada, applied to Captain Juan Joseph Lobato, *the alcalde mayor y capitán de guerra* (principal alcalde and war captain) of the Santa Cruz jurisdiction, for registration of a new brand. Lobato approved the application and authorized Valdes y Bustos to utilize the brand to legally "mark" his livestock. The few examples we have of recorded brands, however, are not all from formal registrations of this type. The brand of Juan Gabaldón, for example, shows up in the 1738 estate papers of Cristóbal Domínguez, which include a formal claim by Gabaldón for return of a mule found among the livestock inventoried with Dominguez' estate.

Several colonial period brand registrations are found in the Spanish Archives of New Mexico in a ledger prepared under the administration of Governor Juan Bautista de Anza and cited as Twitchell #1261 in the Microfilm Edition of the *Land Records of New Mexico* mentioned in the Introduction. Applications for and approval of twenty brands were recorded in this book between June 30, 1781 and October 26, 1785. Each brand is recorded along the margin of the individual brand registrations.

This particular book of brand registrations may have had its origin in an order issued by Governor Anza on March 13, 1784. That day, Anza, with all the formality required by the due process of the day, forwarded a January 15, 1783, order received from the *comandante general* (commanding general) in Chihuahua. The order authorized Anza to issue licenses to the owners and raisers of livestock so that each one could select a brand "for the just concept of avoiding the difficulties…due to the lack of a formalized process …for branding livestock [in New Mexico]." The order specified that all livestock owners were to present the governor or other local officials with documentation of the brands they wanted to use. All approved brands were to be recorded in books maintained by these officials.

Anza ordered local officials to present these brand registers in Santa Fe so he could have a copy made for the archives "so that at no time in the future or under any circumstances no one else may utilize them." He also specified that the order was to be published in all of New Mexico's jurisdictions and towns, including all the Indians settlements, so that it would "have the desired compliance and come to the attention of all the inhabitants of this province." Anza then listed the *cordillera,* or routing of the order, along the margin of the document. After the order was read at each of the political jurisdictions listed, the corresponding local official certified that it was properly published and forwarded to the next jurisdiction listed on the *cordillera.* After the order made its way to the final site listed, it was returned to Santa Fe for archiving in its "proper place."

In the story that follows, we can track Anza's order as the document made its way from the *villa de Santa Fe* along its *cordillera,* or route, to Santa Cruz de la Cañada, Taos, and then south to the *alcaldías* of Queres, Alameda, Alburquerque, Laguna, and Paso del Norte, before being returned to the capital city six months later.

Publication of a Royal Order

Among the many duties of the governor and other local officials of the Spanish colonial system was the proper distribution and publication of royal orders, or *bandos,* in the *alcaldías* and towns of the province. In our electronic society we simply attach an announcement or publication to an email and send a copy to everyone on our list. What takes us a moment to accomplish often took weeks and months in colonial New Mexico. In our previous story, we reviewed Governor Juan Bautista de Anza's publication of a *bando* concerning the registration of livestock brands. This story follows that order as it made its way on a six-month journey through the principal towns of New Mexico.

On March 13, 1784, Governor Anza ordered the distribution and publication of a January 15, 1783, brand registration order he had received from his superiors in Mexico. Local distribution of the order commenced on March 18 with publication of the order in the capital and continued along a specified *cordillera,* or route, with subsequent certifications appended to the same document at each place it was read:

> **Villa de Santa Fe, March 18, 1784**: This order was published by me, Don Antonio José Ortiz, *alcalde mayor* of said *villa,* with the solemnities and customary actions, and I so certify in said *villa* on the said month and year. [Signed] Antonio José Ortiz;
>
> **Villa de Santa Cruz de la Cañada**, [date illegible] …under

my charge, with all the customary solemnities, and to certify, I sign, [signed] José Campo Redondo;

San Geronimo de Taos, April 6, 1784: In obedience to that ordered in the antecedent order, I, Don Christoval Vegil (sic), *alcalde mayor* and *capitán de guerra* of said pueblo, I made it public with all the customary solemnities, and so to certify, I signed [signed] Christobal Vegil;

Pueblo of Santo Domingo, April 24, 1784: In obedience to that ordered in the antecedent *bando*, I Don Antonio de Armenta, *alcalde mayor y capitán de guerra* of said pueblo, published it in this and the rest [of the settlements] of which I am in charge with all said customary solemnities, [signed] Antonio de Armenta;

Pueblo of San Carlos de la Alameda, May 7, 1784: In obedience of the order in the antecedent *bando*, I, the *alcalde mayor y capitán de guerra*, Don Nereo Montoya, made to be published the said with all the customary formalities in all the precincts under my charge, [signed] Nereo Antonio Montoya;

Villa of Alburquerque, May 11, 1784: In obedience [illegible] ordered in the antecedent *bando*, I, the *alcalde mayor y capitán de guerra* of said villa Don Manuel de Arteaga, caused it to be published in the said *villa* and the other precincts under my charge with the customary solemnities, [signed] Manuel de Arteaga;

In this **Pueblo of San José de la Laguna, July 9, 1784**: The antecedent *bando* was published with all the customary formalities, and so to certify its compliance within the jurisdiction under my charge, [signed] Francisco Lobera, *alcalde mayor*;

Pueblo of Our Lady of Guadalupe of El Paso, August 22, 1784: Today on the said date the antecedent *bando* was published in this pueblo with the customary formalities, and I

> ordered the other judicial officers of this jurisdiction do the same in the areas under their charge with the customary statements that they have complied, and so that all is certified, I made this by formal announcement that I sign with my assisting witnesses with whom I act as receiving judge for lack of public or royal scribes, of which there are none [signed] Eugenio Fernandez, Juan Mateo Miranda (asst.) and Miguel Noriega (asst.);

Here follows four virtually identical certifications at the communities associated with the Paso del Norte jurisdiction, dated September 8 through September 21, 1784:

Pueblo de San Lorenzo el Real, by Diego Candelaria;
Pueblo de San Antonio de Senecu, by Manuel Bernadino Borrego;
Pueblo de San Antonio de Corpus Christi de La Isleta, by José María Duran;
Pueblo de Nuestra Señora de La Purisima Concepción del Socorro, by Vicente López.

The document does not have an entry noting when it was received back in Santa Fe. Typically, the last entry would have indicated when it was received and archived for future reference. We can only speculate that officials in El Paso returned the document to Santa Fe with the next mail, which would have been within a month or so after the final certification on September 21 at the pueblo of Socorro. Return of the document would complete a route that took more than six months to make its course. While this may seem to us an inordinate amount of time to complete an important task, it is clear that New Mexican officials carried out Governor Anza's order with deliberation and proper attention to due process.

Pensions for Widows and Orphans

Two centuries ago, at a time in our history that had few of the social "safety nets" we take for granted, it is interesting to see how the Spanish government took care of the widows and orphans of military personnel that died in service to their country. Several documents in the Spanish Archives of New Mexico allow us to trace the process by which this important economic and social act of charity was accomplished.

An example of how the process worked comes from a petition submitted on January 13, 1790 by Governor Fernando Concha to his superior, Pedro de Nava, in Chihuahua. The petition was from María Luisa Tenorio, the widow of Josef Maldonado, a soldier who had also served as the *abilitado*, or quartermaster, of the Santa Fe *presidio* company. The petition was a formal request for payment of two months back pay due Maldonado at the time of his death as well as a pension for the widow. Governor Concha pointed out Maldonado had served the King for more than thirty- two years and the widow's dire need to provide for her family.

Pedro de Nava responded in a letter dated July 26, 1791, returning the petition without taking any action and noting Concha had submitted two disparate issues that had to be resubmitted separately and in a more formal manner. Nava indicated that the request for back pay had to be separated from the petition for a pension and explained that while the widow had no inherent right to a pension, she could petition the King directly, and that he may generously concede such a pension if it was his wish to do so. There is, unfortunately, no record of whether Maldonado's widow followed-up with these requests.

Other cases, however, are more complete. On February 15, 1793, Pedro de Nava wrote to Governor Concha advising him that the *abilitado* (presidio quartermaster), Vicente Troncoso, had died suddenly on December 24, 1792, while conducting *presidio* business in Chihuahua. Two months later, probably within days of when news of Troncoso's death arrived in Santa Fe, Governor Concha advised Nava that Troncoso had left behind a widow, María Ignacia Bernal, who just happened to be the niece of former governor Juan Bautista de Anza. Concha emphasized that four surviving daughters and a son were in a "deplorable" state of need and since Troncoso had died while on duty, he asked Nava to refer the case to the King for consideration "of his mercy and charity."

The king's mercy, however, took a substantial amount of time. On November 17, 1794, more than a year and a half after Governor Concha had petitioned the King, Nava finally notified Concha that as per royal order of July 12 of that year, the King had conceded María Ignacia and her children an annual pension of 120 pesos.

Orphans also received this august consideration. On October 19, 1789, the soldier Alejandro Ortiz was killed during an Apache campaign to the Sierra Obscura in south-central New Mexico. The following month, Governor Concha submitted a report of the campaign and notified his superiors of Ortiz' death. In the report, Concha pointed out that Ortiz, a widower, had left behind a daughter, aged three or four, and apparently because she had no other family, he was personally proving her a stipend of four pesos a month for her subsistence. Concha requested the report be forwarded to the King with an appeal that the young girl be granted a small pension. A little over a year later, Pedro de Nava informed Concha that the King had conceded a pension of eight pesos a month to the orphaned daughter of Alejandro Ortiz. The pension was to be paid until she attained adulthood and included a suggestion that arrangements be made for the girl to be placed under the care of some ecclesiastical authority or other arrangements be made to assure she received a proper education.

The story does not end there. Thirteen years later, on August 22, 1803, Pedro Bautista Pino, the senior *alcalde* of Santa Fe, remitted a report that a young woman named María Dolores Ortiz was to marry Antonio Varela of the "plaza de San Andres de los Padillas," a community located in the outskirts of Alburquerque. Pino noted that María Dolores was the daughter of the deceased soldier Alejandro Ortiz and that she had been receiving a pension of eight pesos a month from the King. His report concluded that in consequence of her betrothal, the pension would be terminated effective August 22, and that she would receive a prorated payment for that year only up to that date. María Dolores' marriage to Antonio Barela is recorded on September 12, 1803, at Santa Fe, and concludes the story of an orphaned child whose life was improved by the benevolence of a distant Sovereign who recognized the sacrifice her father made while fighting the Crown's enemies.

Urban Renewal in Santa Fe, 1790

Visitors and long-time Santa Fe residents often ask, "What did the plaza look like in the old days?" When confronted with this question, my response includes three basic facts: first, the historic plaza is as old as the *villa* of Santa Fe, which was established in 1610; second, three centuries ago, the plaza was much larger than it is today; and third, a building on the north side of the plaza, which we have come to know as the Palace of the Governors, was probably in the same general location as it is today. Aside from these basic facts, the rest of my response concludes with, "But we don't really know."

There is a general lack of information about Santa Fe's first one hundred and fifty years that makes it difficult to develop an accurate idea of what the old plaza (or Santa Fe itself, for that matter) may have looked like. If there were early detailed descriptions of Santa Fe and its buildings, they apparently disappeared during the Revolt of 1680, when all the documents in the Spanish archives were destroyed. Between 1680 and 1692, it is likely that virtually every building in the city was modified significantly, if not destroyed, by the Pueblo Indians who occupied Santa Fe. When Diego de Vargas and the Spanish returned in 1692, they in turn demolished or modified what the Pueblos had built, and constructed a new Santa Fe.

Through the centuries, the plaza and downtown Santa Fe underwent slow, and occasionally, dramatic changes. One of the most dramatic changes took place during a four-year period that began in 1788. That year, New Mexico Governor Fernando de la Concha announced plans to relocate the Santa Fe *presidio.* His plans called for construction of new buildings in which to consolidate housing for the *presidio* troops and their families at a site outside the plaza area. Sites considered included the Barrio del Analco, located along the southern bank of the Santa Fe River, as well as a site near Santo Domingo Pueblo. These proposals were dropped when the Pueblo protested about encroachment on their land, and Santa Fe residents complained about having the troops stationed twenty miles from the capital. Instead, plans were made to construction the new *presidio* building on the land adjacent to the north of the plaza. Surviving reports on the project provide details about what was accomplished.

Preparations for construction of the new *quartel* probably began the spring of 1788, after Treasury officials at Chihuahua confirmed they had budgeting 2000 *pesos* for the project. By January 1879, Governor de la Concha reported lumber had been cut and stacked, straw and other materials gathered, and that they were ready to begin making adobes that upcoming spring. With this news, officials in Chihuahua authorized an additional 4,000 pesos, but cautioned economy and moderation in purchases of materials.

On March 27, 1789, Governor de la Concha issued a *bando*, or order, that instructed the *alcaldes* of surrounding communities to prepare lists of all men ages 16 through 50, who would be eligible to work on construction of the new building. Exemptions were allowed for all those individuals who had their own land to cultivate and could support their families, as well as those who were already gainfully employed. Unfortunately, there are no surviving lists of those who reported to work on the project.

By November 1790, the project was nearly completed. The governor reported it had been an unusually wet summer, and torrential rains hindered work on several occasions. One devastating downpour reportedly destroyed nearly 80,000 adobes. Despite these setbacks, ninety eight of the planned 114 houses were completed and soon inhabited by *presidio* soldiers and their families.

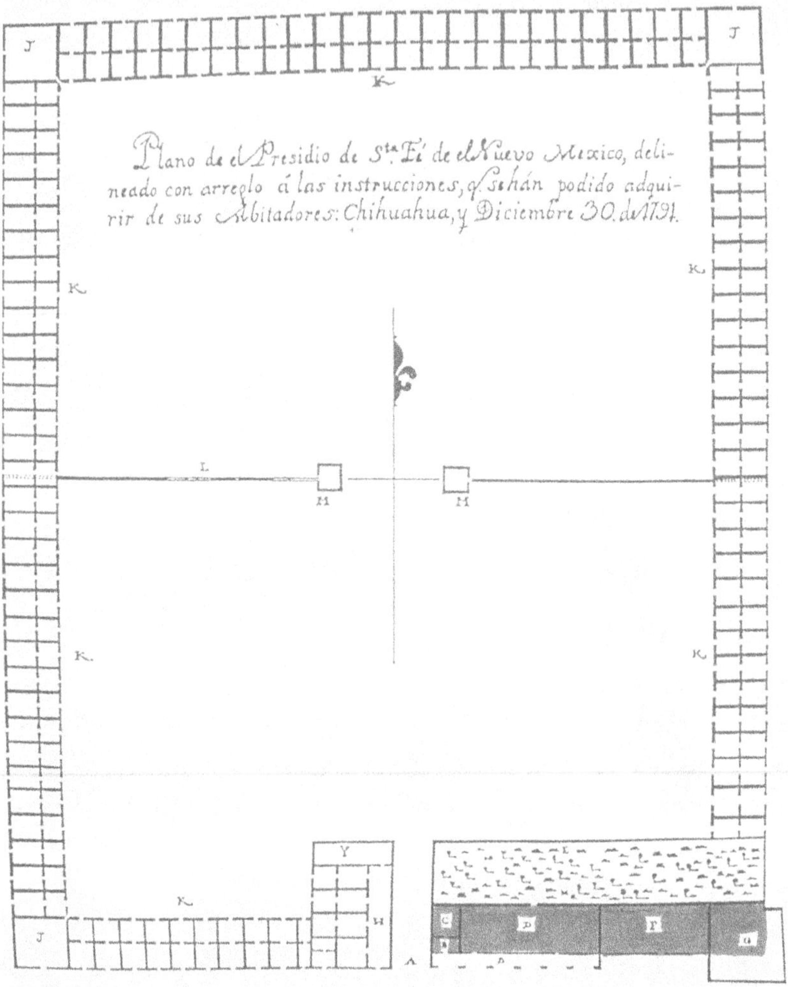

Plan of Santa Fe Presidio quartel, 1791. The shaded area corresponds to today's Palace of the Governors. AGN, Provincias Internas de Nuevo Mexico, 1763-1992 (Tomo 161). Microfilm at New Mexico State Records Center and Archives.

Governor Concha's final report of October 31, 1791, shows total cost of the project was more than 22,000 *pesos*. More than 9,000 *pesos* were cash expenditures, and the balance was paid with "*efectos a pesos de la tierra*," cash equivalents in products of the land. Concha's report indicates that in addition to the nearly 7,000 *pesos* received from the treasury in Chihuahua, the project was financed from donations and sale of surplus equipment and supplies.

These included a personal donation of 938 *pesos* from the governor and 366 *pesos* from other high-ranking government officials.

This was a massive building project. Nearly one hundred new residential units were added to the vicinity of Santa Fe's plaza, undoubtedly contributing to a drastic change in the appearance of the city. The accompanying illustration shows what the completed *quartel* may have looked like. Of the buildings constructed more than two hundred years ago, only that part we know as the Palace of the Governors exists today. We can only imagine what the city would look like if other portions of these buildings had survived to become part of the fabric of what we now know as downtown Santa Fe.

The Comanche Raid of 1776

When one considers the extraordinary documentary legacy left by the Spanish colonial government, one might be surprised to find out that the Spanish civil government did not record births, marriages and deaths. In the absence of this type of civil records for New Mexico's Spanish (1598-1821), Mexican (1821-1846), and most of our Territorial period (1846-1912), the sacramental records of the Catholic Archdiocese of Santa Fe become the principal source of information for these most basic human activities.

There are numerous serious incidents recorded in church records for which there is no corresponding documentation in New Mexico's Spanish and Mexican archives. One of the most stunning examples of this is found in nine burials recorded more than two centuries ago in Santa Fe between June 21 and June 23, 1776. Each burial has a nearly identical notation that each of the individuals buried on those days had died "at the hands of Comanche" when the raiders apparently swept through the community of La Cienega and the nearby settlement of Cienegilla, both located less than ten miles south of Santa Fe. There is no corresponding report of this incident in the surviving Spanish government records, so we know little else about the incident.

These nine burials, however, as well as a number of subsequent entries in this particular book of burials, provide us an extraordinary amount of information about the individuals killed in the raid. These entries contain much more that the basic facts of name, date and site of burial. They include information about where the men lived, the type of work they were doing when killed, their parents, race, marital and social status. If they were married, the name of the widow and number of surviving children is included. These entries then proceed to note the location where each individual is buried within the parish church in Santa Fe as well as the amount and manner of payment made for each burial and associated services.

The burial record of Julian Valenzuela is typical of these:

> On the twenty-first of June 1776, I gave ecclesiastic burial to Julian Valenzuela, a native of this *villa* of Santa Fe, single, a member of this church, Spanish, legitimate son of Juan Francisco Valenzuela and Felipa Ortega… Said Julian Valenzuela died at the hands of the Comanche Thursday, the twentieth of this June at the *puesto* of la Cienega without having received any sacraments, and is buried about two *varas* in front of the altar of the Holy Sepulcher as you walk on the left towards the door of the church. His father gave, or has agreed to give, for the opening of the grave, five pesos of produce from the land, and the burial was made without charge. So that it is valid, I signed this on the said day, month, and year… Fray Francisco Atanacio Dominguez.

The subsequent entries record similar information on Christóbal Martín, a widower with eight surviving children; Santiago Mascareñas, single; Domingo Romero, single; Domingo de Ortega, married; José Vicente, single; José Vicente, single; Manuel de Coca (Coza?), married, and José Antonio Sandoval, a young boy.

This treasure trove of genealogical and historical information is unusual by most standards, but understandable considering the individual who made the entries. This portion of the burial records for Santa Fe are recorded by the imminent Fray Francisco Atanacio Domínguez, who was in New Mexico at this point in history to participate in the subsequent journey of exploration that is commonly known as the Domínguez-Escalante Expedition of 1776. Fray Domínguez was also here in the role of a Visitor General on behalf of the Bishop of Durango, inspecting the New Mexico missions and examining the sacramental books. His entry in the Santa Fe books immediately preceding the burial entries of the nine men described above specifies that although the entries to that point were "adequate," they needed to conform more closely to edicts issued in 1775 by the Bishop of Durango. No doubt, his own extensive entries were to serve as an example of how subsequent entries should be made

The admonitions apparently worked, at least for a time. For nearly a year afterwards, the entries made by Fray José Medrano, the pastor at Santa Fe's *parroquia*, or parish church, generally contain much more information than they did earlier. However, they slowly diminish in length and by the early 1780s consist of little more than four or five lines of very basic information. For this period, however, we can be thankful for the vast amount of information we can glean from these burial entries. They not only tell us of the Comanche raid itself, but that the losses sustained in the raid consisted of much more than mere numbers of individuals killed.

A Bridge Over the Rio Grande

The Spanish Archives of New Mexico contain a number of documents related to construction of bridges over the Rio del Norte, as the Rio Grande was generally know, at the crossing of the river at El Paso del Norte, between present day El Paso, Texas, and Cuidad Júarez. One of the earliest mentions of these projects is from the summer of 1797, when Francisco Xavier Bernal reported problems associated with the delivery of timber for the bridge. In June 1797, Bernal reported that fifty-five men had been sent north from El Paso del Norte to pick up lumber sent from an unspecified location in New Mexico.

The lumber was apparently transported by lashing it together and floating it down the Rio Grande. The process nearly met with disaster when the raft of lumber broke apart along the stretch of the river that parallels the *jornada del muerto* in southern New Mexico. When the raft overturned, the escort lost all its provisions and had to abandon the lumber and proceed to El Paso to re-supply. They returned later that month to reconstruct the raft and complete the journey.

During the following several months, correspondence and reports show that bridge construction was delayed by a shortage of funds and squabbles regarding who was responsible for a number of associated expenses. *Comandante general* Pedro de Nava felt that two hundred pesos needed to complete the project should be contributed by those merchants and traders who benefited the most from the new bridge. In November 1798, New Mexico governor Fernando Chacón settled the issue when he volunteered to provide the funds from his own pocket.

The reasons are not specified, but work on the bridge was delayed further for more than a year. Finally, in early summer 1800, Governor Chacón noted that a work force of eighty-seven men, consisting of a troop escort, *vecinos* and Indians, were on the way to El Paso del Norte with a new shipment of lumber. In August, Chacón personally traveled to El Paso del Norte and stayed there until late October to supervise the bridge project.

Chacón's reports indicate a number of problems caused by the constant rising and falling water levels. Despite the problems and delays, the bridge was reported completed on October 15, 1800. Chacón indicated the new bridge was located at the same site as the "old" one, and had utilized foundations left behind by flooding that apparently swept away the earlier bridge. The new bridge, located one-half league north of the settlements at the traditional crossing of the river, was five *varas* wide (approximately fourteen feet) and one hundred and fifty *varas* long (nearly 420 feet). A smaller bridge over the *acequia* that paralleled the river had also been completed. Trees and other vegetation planted along both ends of the bridge formed a "peaceful site for rest and recreation."

Over the next several years, *vigas* and lumber were regularly sent to El Paso del Norte to repair and reinforce the bridge. On June 14, 1802, for example, a party of New Mexicans delivered fifty-two *vigas* for that purpose. The lumber was delivered with instructions that it was to be securely stored. This type of lumber was highly sought after for the construction of window sashes, doors, tables, benches, and other furniture, and Governor Chacón wanted to make sure it did not disappear as had some from earlier deliveries.

Bridge over the Rio Grande at San Felipe. Photostint/ Fred Harvey PC. Robert J, Tórrez Collection.

Timber from New Mexico was regularly sent to El Paso for bridge repairs and maintenance due to constant damage inflicted on the structure by the turbulent waters of the Rio Grande. By 1816, for example, another new bridge was reported completed. This constant need of repairs and rebuilding imposed severe hardships on settlements as far north as Taos. In the spring of 1819, Taos residents protested an order to provide forty yoke of oxen to gather and deliver *vigas* to the Rio Grande for shipment to El Paso del Norte. They felt the order was badly timed because their oxen were barely recovering from the winter and were needed locally to plow the fields. Governor Facundo Melgares agreed and ordered the delivery suspended.

Despite these documented efforts to build bridges over the Rio Grande at El Paso del Norte, none apparently lasted very long. By the mid 1820s, the bridge was apparently in bad condition or had been swept away because boats or rafts were being utilized to ferry goods across the river. The archives do not reflect when the next new bridge was constructed across this historic crossing of our Rio Grande.

The Iturbide Celebration of 1822

Agustín de Iturbide. Wikimedia/commons.

The archives from New Mexico's late Spanish and early Mexican period make it clear that despite New Mexico's relative isolation along New Spain's northernmost frontier, local officials were kept well informed of developments while Mexico made its often painful journey towards independence from Spain. Within weeks of the events that resulted in Mexican independence, Governor Facundo Melgares was distributing the latest news to local officials throughout the territory. So it was when Agustín de Iturbide proclaimed himself Imperial Emperor as 1821 came to a close. In December 1822, officials in Santa Fe organized a grand celebration to commemorate the first anniversary of Iturbide's inauguration as "first Mexican constitutional emperor."

The Iturbide celebration opened in Santa Fe the evening of December 10, 1822. The occasion was marked by prayers, bonfires, music, ringing of bells, and discharges of artillery and firearms. A white flag emblazoned with unspecified "inscriptions of independence" was hoisted on a very tall pole erected at the center of the plaza. Later that night, Governor José Antonio Viscarra and Lt. Colonel José Antonio Arze led a parade through the streets accompanied by a musical troupe, singing songs "appropriate to the occasion." Shouts of "*viva el emperador*" punctuated the cold December night until two in the morning.

The celebration continued on December 11 before sunrise with artillery salvos and a parade through the streets. At nine in the morning, a Mass was sung at the parish church and a patriotic sermon delivered by the Rev. Francisco Rada, pastor of Santa Cruz de la Cañada. At four in the afternoon, the Imperial Standard was brought out from the parish church in a fabulous procession led by a young boy dressed as an angel. The boy held a sword in his hand and was followed by a second boy dressed in black, representing Padre Miguel Hidalgo. Don Pedro Armendaris, the *alférez público,* followed on horseback with the "Imperial Standard" of the Emperor. Provincial delegates Juan Vigil and Agapito Alva, *primer alcalde* of Santa Fe, José Francisco Baca, and Santiago Abreu, *procurador sindico* [district attorney] followed.

The procession of dignitaries was followed by an elaborately adorned cart in which a young girl representing Liberty was seated. Two women, one representing North America and the other, South America, stood at her side, both connected to Liberty by a sash. Slightly above and behind Liberty was a bust of the Emperor with a young girl representing Justice holding a silver crown in both hands, as if crowning the emperor. At the rear marched musicians and the *alférez* Felipe Griego with an escort of forty soldiers in column and sixteen elaborately dressed young boys and girls in two files, each wearing a sash of ribbon on which was written "*viva el Emperador.*" Behind them followed two troupes of *matachines,* one composed of children and another of adult men. Seven groups from the various Pueblos danced along the route of the procession.

The parade continued to the plaza, where the *alférez público* set the Imperial Standard on a platform erected near the entrance to the corridor of the *palacio* (Palace of the Governors) facing the *plaza mayor.* As soon as Armendaris stepped down from the platform, the public celebration began as the Pueblo Indians and *matachines* danced and table games opened.

That night a theatre was set up on the plaza and an *opera* (a musical performance) presented that featured three principal characters. Don José María Baca, secretary of the *ayuntamiento* (municipal council), portrayed the King of Spain, the *alférez* Felipe Griego, the king's Minister of State, and Santiago Abreu, the Mexican Ambassador. A dance followed at the governor's residence, "in which gentlemen and ladies offered toasts in the name of the Emperor, and every song and shout was directed to his honor."

The following day, December 12, the governor and local officials took an oath of allegiance to Iturbide as "First Mexican Emperor" at an altar that was erected next to the platform on which the Imperial Standard had been placed the previous day. At the conclusion of these ceremonies, dances and other festivities continued until seven that night when a colloquy in honor of Our Lady of Guadalupe was presented (it was, after all, December 12). This was followed by a "discourse between Moors and Christians" and a presentation by the children's *matachines.* A formal ball followed at the house of don Juan Pino. The following day, another procession was held, followed by patriotic speeches, music, and a comedy prepared by don Domingo Fernandes. An evening dance held at the house of don Atanacio Bolivar concluded the festivities.

Within three months of this celebration New Mexico received communications from Mexico advising that Iturbide had been deposed as emperor. His short-lived reign as Emperor of Mexico, however, left us with a fascinating record of three days of enthusiastic celebration that marked one of New Mexico's first documented observations of Mexican independence from Spain.

The Royal Contribution of 1809

During the Spanish colonial period, it was a fairly common practice for the King to ask his subjects for donations to supplement the expenses of government operations. New Mexico responded to these requests along with the rest of the Spanish empire. The Spanish Archives of New Mexico contain a fascinating document which describes part of the contribution our ancestors made in response to one such request in 1809.

In April 1809, Cleto Miera y Pacheco, the *alcalde* at San Carlos de la Alameda, submitted a detailed list of the donations made from his district, which extended from Alameda north to Peña Blanca. The list is twenty pages long and contains the names of approximately 700 individuals who pledged a contribution to the Royal government.

The list includes cash donations which range from the 11 *pesos* given by Dionicio Gonzales of Corrales, to one *real* (there are 8 *reales* to the *peso*) contributed by Bartolo Chaves of Bernalillo. The contributions include blankets, a variety of crops, several types of cloth, and livestock of all descriptions. The following is a small sample of the contributions listed for each town:

> **From Alameda**: Alcalde Don Cleto Miera y Pacheco... 10 *pesos* in cash (noted as *en reales*); Felix Pino... 1 mule; Eusebio Real... 1 *sarape* and 9 *reales*; Felipe Montoya... an ox and an yearling burro; Miguel Garcia... a *sarape*, a two year old bull and half a *fanega* of corn (a *fanega* is approximately 2 1/2 bushels).

From Corrales: Juan Gonzales... a two year old mare; Diego Lucero... 1 yearling calf and a 3 pesos cash; Miguel Garcia... 6 *varas* (an official measure of approximately thirty-three inches) of *gerga* (a coarse cloth commonly used as a floor covering, like carpet);

From Bernalillo: Mariano Perea... a year old mule and a calf; Andres Romero... 10 *pesos* in cash; Juan Domingo Archibeque... 1 calf, 1 *sarape*, and 1 *peso.*

From Peña Blanca: José de la Cruz Crespin... 2 *sarapes*; Juan Leiva... 2 *pesos* in cash; Juan Apodaca... 3 *almures* (12 *almures* make 1 *fanega*) of corn; Don Luis María Cabesa de Baca..... a mule.

From Rancho de Santa Barbara de Chile: Juan Lucero... a two year old bull; José Archiveque... a mare.

From Canada de Cochiti: Christóbal Lucero... 1 *sarape* and 1 pair of stockings; Cruz Padilla... 2 *fanegas* of corn; Ysidro Hurtado... 1 *gamusa* (a soft tanned hide like chamois).

From the Pueblo of Nuestra Señora de Los Dolores de Sandia: Governor Juan... 1 *manta* (a cotton or woolen cloth) and one *jicara* (probably a reed basket); Vicente Conejo... 4 pesos in cash; José Antonio... 1 buffalo hide; Asencio... 1 *manta* and 3 *almures* of beans.

From Pueblo of San Felipe: Governor José Riano... 4 *reales*, 1 *sarape*, and one gamusa; Juan Rosalio... 1 *sarape* and 3 *almures* of corn; Joaquin Velasquez... 2 rams and 1 *peso*; Juan Sanches... 1 *sarape* and 1 ram.

From Pueblo of Santo Domingo: Governor Agustín... 7 *reales*, 1 *sarape*, and 3 *almures* of corn; Juan Domingo Coris..... 3 *almures* of corn and 2 *ristras* of garlic; José Tomas... 1/2 fanega of corn and 1 *ristra* of *chile*; Ambrosio... 1 *almud* of peas and 1 *ristra* of garlic.

> **From Pueblo of San Buenaventura de Cochiti**: Governor Santiago... 2 *sarapes*; Leonardo Coris... 1 buffalo hide and 3 *almures* of beans; Geronimo Sanches... 1 *fanega* of corn.

The money and goods contributed totaled 117 pesos, 2 1/2 *reales* in cash; 218 *sarapes*; more than 160 *almures* of corn, wheat and assorted legumes; livestock which included 49 cattle, 4 mules, 7 horses and 2 burros; 22 buffalo hides; clothing, including 6 pairs of stockings, 3 pairs of boots and 14 sashes; several dozen *varas* of various types of cloth; 18 *ristras* of *chile*, and 38 *ristras* of garlic.

There were various other items contributed, some of which have not yet been positively identified. The most interesting of these are the dozen or so *congas*, which may have been black faced or dark fleeced sheep. These donations provide us an interesting look at the past by showing us the type of goods and livestock people of that era owned, and also give us a peak at what these individuals felt they could afford to contribute to the support of the Spanish king.

The Salt Caravans

The Spanish came to New Mexico in the sixteenth century looking for converts to Christianity and for minerals that would enrich them personally and fill the coffers of the Spanish kings. The search for silver, gold, mercury and other valuable minerals during the subsequent centuries proved fruitless. Yet, New Mexico abounded in a mineral that one might not think of as valuable – salt.

Salt is essential to life, and New Mexico is blessed with a plentiful supply of this readily obtainable mineral from the famous saline lakes of the Estancia Valley east of the Manzano Mountains. These *salinas*, or salt beds, have been a source of this essential mineral for centuries. Long before the Spanish came to this New World, the Estancia Valley and its ancient salt lakes were utilized by native peoples from throughout the region. The Pueblos came from the north and west, the various plains tribes from the east and northeast, and from the south, the Jumanos and others from Mexico. Over the centuries, this area was probably a point of cultural contact for these peoples, and the salt trade may have served as a catalyst for periodic trade between the groups that traveled there. By the fourteenth century, the Piros of the southern New Mexico Pueblos established themselves in the region and developed a series of settlements that we have come to identify as the Salinas Pueblos.

These pueblo peoples learned to harvest high-quality salt and built a trade network that allowed them to grow and prosper. One source estimated their trade networks extended south as far as present-day Chihuahua and as far north as Taos. By the time the Spanish made their way into the Estancia

Valley there were at least ten Salinas pueblos with a population of several thousand.

Arrival of the Spanish brought significant changes to the Salinas. During the seventeenth century, Spanish Franciscans established six missions among these pueblos. The ruins of three of these, Abo, Gran Quivira, and Quarai, stand as witness to the grand scale of these missionary efforts. Spanish rule, however, also had other effects on the pueblos and the salt trade. Spanish colonization greatly increased the magnitude of the trade, not only for table use, but for livestock and industrial uses, such as the curing of hides for leather. During the later part of the seventeenth century, Spanish governors were sending caravans laden with salt as far as the silver mines of Parral.

A devastating drought and a series of man-caused disasters during the late 1600s led to the abandonment of the Salinas pueblos by the time of the Pueblo Revolt of 1680. Although the region would not be resettled until the late eighteenth century, the need for salt continued, and during the early 1700s, the Spanish government established a system of annual escorted caravans to harvest this valuable resource. One of the earliest documents from our Spanish Archives that describes this process is a 1716 *bando* issued by Governor Felix Martínez announcing the departure of a military escort to the *salinas* on or about July 20th. The announcement orders the *alcaldes* of the various jurisdictions to advise all the residents of the province that anyone who wanted to join the caravan could do so.

Quari Mission, Salinas National Monument. No photographer noted.

A similar order issued by Governor Domingo de Bustamante in 1730 advised that a squad of soldiers from the *presidio* had been assigned to escort a caravan scheduled to gather at the Pueblo of Galisteo on June 9, "from where all shall leave together to said *salinas*." A number of documents show this procedure was followed, probably on an annual basis, for several decades. The wording of one such order, issued by Governor Joaquin Codallos y Rabal on August 27, 1748, is noteworthy in its explanation of the process:

> Because the time has arrived when we can go to the Salinas for salt for the maintenance and use of Spanish residents and Indians of this kingdom, as has been customary: I order the *alcaldes mayores*, and in their absence, their assistants, each in their respective jurisdictions, publish this order for said residents and Indians so they may be prepared, on the sixth of September of this year, that at the Pueblo of Galisteo, there will be a squad of soldiers of this royal *presidio* to serve as an escort to and from said *salinas.*

The order then specified the customary certification of the publication at each of the jurisdictions. Unfortunately, none of the extant documents tells us much about who went on these salt caravans, their size, or amount of salt extracted. It is likely, however, that a considerable number of individuals gathered on these occasions. One 1808 caravan conducted under command of an individual identified only as "Abeita," consisted of 200 men and 400 mules.

The *salinas* of the Estancia Valley continued to produce salt commercially until nearly the middle of the twentieth century. When the last of these enterprises closed, it ended more than six centuries of trade in the mineral that benefited every group that has made New Mexico their home.

The Convict Soldier-Colonists of 1677

A most interesting convoy made its way north from Mexico to New Mexico in 1677. The documentation says nothing of the number of wagons, livestock and other accoutrements that would have been constituted such an expedition in that time and place of our history. What made this expedition different was that it consisted of forty-seven men who had been convicted of a variety of crimes and sentenced to royal service in New Mexico for periods of two or more years. The utilization of convicts in this manner was not unusual in the Spanish colonial penal system. The Spanish judicial system did not typically utilize long prison terms as punishments for crimes. Instead, convicts were often sentenced to labor at mills that produced woolen goods called *obrajes* or to serve along the frontier with the military. Interestingly, most (but not all) convicts were sentenced to such labor *with a salary*. The salary paid each of the men in this 1677 group is listed in great detail in the reports.

The men sent to this northernmost outpost of New Mexico were expected to reinforce a frontier colony desperate for help in the "preservation and defense against the many hostilities" of the various Apache tribes that constantly raided the Pueblos and Spanish settlements. The forty- seven convict soldiers, their commanding officer, a sergeant and three volunteer soldiers were sent in hopes of providing a stronger military presence. They also brought one hundred firearms, one hundred hilts for swords and daggers, fifty saddles with bridles and spurs and one thousand horses.

Of course, none of the convicts came north of their free will, so the group dwindled as it made its way north. Joaquin de Rojas y Zapata, who had been ill and allowed to travel without the security of fetters, escaped at Parral and was apparently not seen or heard from again. The remainder of the expedition arrived safely and without incident at the crossing of the Rio del Norte (Rio Grande), where they were delivered to New Mexico Governor Antonio de Otermín. However, swift currents and high water delayed them from crossing the river into New Mexico for an unspecified, but "long" delay. During this period six additional convicts, some of whom had been assigned to guard duty, made their escape. They took with them fifty- seven horses, three *arquebuses,* or muskets, and six saddles.

The remainder eventually made their way to New Mexico. On February 12, 1678, Governor Otermín certified a muster of those who made it to Santa Fe, so they must have arrived shortly before that date. This muster and previous official lists tell us a great deal about these men. These lists provide their names, parents, birthplace, age, and a brief physical description. Typical of these descriptions is that of Lázaro de Mizquia, one of the three volunteer soldiers. He is listed as "son of Domingo, native of the villa of Motrico in the province of Guipuzoca, twenty-four years of age, very tall, fair, with a broad face, large forehead, and thick eyebrows..." None of the descriptions list the specific crime for which these men were condemned by the courts, but their term of service and the amount each was paid is indicated. Those interested in the full list of these convict soldiers and the details provided for each can find the reports in Volume III of Charles Wilson Hackett (editor), *Historical Documents related to New Mexico, Nueva Vizcaya, and Approaches Thereto, to 1773.*

This group of soldier colonists was relatively young. Three of the youngest, including brothers Juan and Eusebio Blanco of Xalpa, were only fifteen. Five others were seventeen and eighteen, while the oldest, Bernardo de la Fuente and Domingo García, were forty- eight and fifty, respectively. Two young men, Antonio de Barbas, age twenty-one, and Francisco de Velasco, eighteen, are identified as *Bachiller*, indicating they may have had a university education. Both were condemned by an ecclesiastical court for unspecified offenses.

Most of these men disappear from the historical record within a few years. Most were gone from New Mexico when the Pueblo Revolt erupted in 1680 because their terms of service had expired and these presumably chose to return to their homes in Mexico. A few, however, remained in New Mexico and are listed by Fray Angélico Chávez in *Origins of New Mexico Families.* Marcos Ramos, for example, was killed at the Pueblo of Santa Clara on August 10, 1680, at the outbreak of the revolt. Others, such as Francisco Rascón, escaped to Paso del Norte with the retreating colonists and made a life for himself in the surrounding settlements. It does not appear that any of the convict soldiers sent to New Mexico in 1677 returned to the province with Diego de Vargas following the re-conquest of 1692-1693. A more careful examination of historical records may, however, reveal that some of these convict soldiers made more than a passing contribution to the history of New Mexico.

The Smallpox Epidemic of 1780-81

It never seems to fail. Every time one begins to search through a particular collection of documents in the Spanish or Mexican Archives of New Mexico, we are distracted from what we are actually looking for by some unrelated but fascinating reference. Such was the case as I was looking through the muster of the Santa Fe presidio troops for March 1, 1781. This particular document notes that twenty-seven of the troops, almost a fourth of the total strength of one hundred twenty men, were sick. A significant portion of the troops had fallen victim to the most dreaded disease of the time. *La virguela*, or small pox, was sweeping the territory.

This deadly epidemic had apparently begun during the late spring of 1780, when a number of deaths from the disease were recorded in the burial records of Alburquerque and other communities in the territory. By the fall of 1780, it appeared the worst was over, but the several dozen deaths recorded that year were only a portent of the terrible impact the disease would have on New Mexico the following year.

The early signs of the extent of *la virguela* show up in the burial records of the parish church in Santa Fe as well as other missions in early January 1781. The entries, beginning January 5 for the *parroquia*, or parish church of Santa Fe, consist of several pages of burials through early March, when the records show a return to a semblance of normalcy. In January, Fray José de Burgos lists burials of forty-one men, women and children, with the worst yet to come. In February the burials increased more than four-fold with a total of 181 burials for that month alone. The crest of the epidemic was reached in mid-February. On the 19th Fray Burgos made his final entries with the twelve burials he conducted that day.

As of February 20, Fray Burgos no longer made entries into the parish records of the *parroquia*. Instead, Fray Juan Bermejo, the *capellan*, or chaplain of the *castrense*, the soldier's chapel located on the south side of the plaza in Santa Fe, took over the daunting task, apparently by himself. By the following day, February 21, Fray Bermejo discontinued listing the burials individually as he noted in obvious desperation, "On this day I gave ecclesiastic burial to fifteen souls – ten adults and five children."

The historical record does not account for the sudden disappearance of Fray Burgos from Santa Fe after February 19. It is possible he too succumbed to the dreadful disease that had taken so many of his parishioners. However, there is no burial entry for him among the dozens interred by Fray Bermejo. Burgos may have been reassigned to a nearby mission or may have been sick or simply overwhelmed by the enormity of the circumstances. Regardless, his absence must have imposed an extraordinary burden of Fray Bermejo. One can only image the labor it took to administer dozens of last rites and then conduct graveside services. Bermejo had not only helped his colleague to bury the 230 persons associated with the *parroquia* of Santa Fe, but had also been responsible for a additional 138 burials associated with his primary responsibility, the *castrense*.

The scene in Santa Fe, not to speak of the dozens of communities afflicted throughout the territory, must have been like a scene directly from Dante's Inferno. Considering for a moment the 292 burials recorded at the *parroquia* and *the castrense* for February alone and that there were no burials on only two days that month, means there was an average of more than ten burials a day that month alone - with twelve, fifteen, eighteen, and thirteen burials recorded on February 14, 19, 21, 23, and the 28th, respectively. It is likely that few families were unaffected by this tragic event.

The tragedy was no less in other communities. In one of the few published articles dealing with this topic, Marc Simmons, in a 1966 article in the *New Mexico Historical Review*, notes that the disease probably hit the pueblos even harder than Santa Fe. He lists 130 deaths at San Felipe for February alone; 230 during February and early March at Santo Domingo, and more than 200 at Santa Clara and Cochiti. These include *vecinos,* or Spanish settlers, from the surrounding communities as well as the *indios* of the various pueblos.

Simmons says that Herbert Eugene Bolton claimed more than 5,000 Pueblo Indians died of the disease by the end of 1781. There is no estimate given of how many thousands more of our New Mexican ancestors succumbed to this epidemic. We can only guess how many families may have been wiped out completely; or how many orphans, widowers and widows were left behind to fend as best they could. Those of us who live in an era where the most virulent of diseases have been nearly, if not completely eradicated, can only image the suffering endured by those who died as well as those who survived these most trying times.

Smallpox Immunization Comes to New Mexico

The tragedy of periodic smallpox epidemics in New Mexico such as the 1780-81 epidemic described in the previous story began to be mitigated by an often overlooked, but extraordinarily important event that took place a little over two centuries ago on March 21, 1805. That day, New Mexico took a small but important early step in the heroic efforts that finally eradicated smallpox in the 1970s. Smallpox, a dreaded disease that killed millions throughout history, swept through New Mexico a number of times. Thousands of New Mexicans died during the smallpox epidemic of 1780-81, with nearly two hundred Santa Fe residents succumbing to the dreaded *virguela* in February 1781 alone.

As early as 1803, less than a decade after British physician Edward Jenner proved that inoculation with cowpox provided immunity to smallpox, the Spanish government instituted a formal program to distribute the vaccine throughout its worldwide empire. The first challenge they encountered was how to effectively transport delicate vials of the vaccine across vast oceans, rugged mountain ranges, and arid desserts. This problem was solved by using *in vivo* carriers to transport the antibodies. Sources tells us that groups of orphans were inoculated and transported, along with Spanish physicians, across the Atlantic to serve as live carriers of the vaccine serum.

The Spanish government's immunization program extended even to New Mexico. A May 20, 1804 royal order found in New Mexico's own Spanish archives advises local officials that the smallpox vaccine was on its way and ordered every province to prepare a hall or building where the vaccine was to be kept and conserved after it arrived locally. While there is no indication New Mexican officials ever established such a repository, by August 1804, news arrived in New Mexico that this "marvelous discovery" was being distributed in Chihuahua and ordered the *cirujano*, or military surgeon, Cristóbal Larrañaga, be sent to Chihuahua with the next scheduled caravan. He was to take along six or eight boys so they could serve as *in vivo* carriers of the *fluido*, the live virus that would then be utilized *de brazo á brazo* (from arm to arm) when they return to New Mexico.

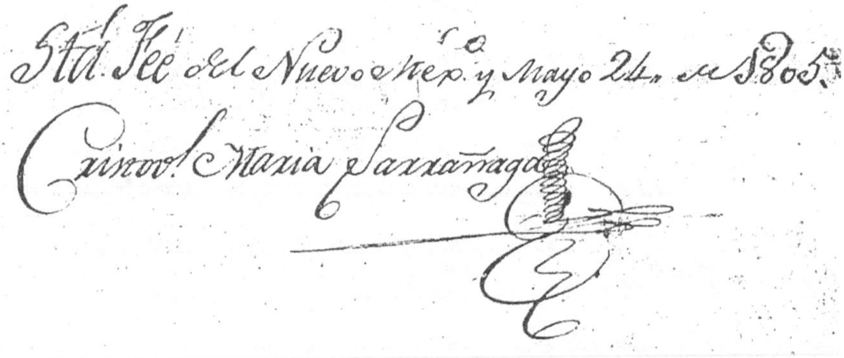

Cristobal Maria Larrañaga signature on his 1805 report on smallpox vaccinations.

The documents do not tell us who these children were, but Larrañaga and the boys chosen for this heroic and very dangerous task must have left to Chihuahua with the caravan that November, and were ready to begin their trip back to New Mexico in early February 1805. On the fifteenth of that month, Governor Joaquín del Real Alencaster was informed that Larrañaga had completed his instruction on the use and propagation of the vaccine, and that an adequate number of boys had been inoculated and were ready to bring the vaccine to New Mexico's communities.

Larrañaga's first report of immunizations in New Mexico is dated March 24, 1805. His report tells us he had vaccinated four children at the Paraje de Valverde south of Socorro on the twelfth of that month and that these four had arrived at Sevilleta "*con el fluido perfectamente clavado.*" This seems to mean that these four had the antibody perfectly developed and provided the *fluido* for the vaccinations that commenced at Sevilleta a quarter after seven the morning of March 21. That day, Larrañaga "performed the operation of vaccination" on twenty-two boys and girls at the home of the unnamed *Sargento Comandate* of that place. He noted that more were not vaccinated because the area was in the midst of a measles (*saranpión*) epidemic and these twenty-two were the only ones not suffering from symptoms at that time. He also noted that a list of the children inoculated at Sevilleta was appended to his report. Unfortunately, the appended list has apparently not survived. If it had, we would know the names of the twenty- two children who were the first recipients of the smallpox vaccination at Sevilleta on that historic day of March 21, 1805.

From Sevilleta, Larrañaga proceeded to Sabinal, where an additional thirty-eight children were vaccinated. He then continued north to the *villa* de Alburquerque and the capital at Santa Fe, where he carried out at least four vaccination sessions. In a report dated May 24, 1805, Larrañaga listed a total of 257 inoculations performed at these sites up to that date. Other reports and lists indicate local surveys were done at that time in order to determine the number of children in other parts of New Mexico that had not acquired smallpox naturally, presumably to determine how much vaccine had to be prepared to proceed with the vaccination program.

In November 1805, Governor Alencaster reported 3,610 vaccinations had been completed throughout New Mexico. During subsequent years, documents show the transport of fresh antibodies and vaccination programs carried out in various parts of New Mexico. A few even include full lists of names of the children vaccinated, their ages and parent's names. While the entire story of this truly heroic vaccination project cannot be detailed here, we can acknowledge the foresight of the Spanish government and the local officials who carried out the inoculations for their part in what one author called "a most important act in the history of public health."

Contract for a Horse Race, 1846

If we look at the official records of government during the spring of 1846, it would seem to have been an anxious time in New Mexico. Tensions were mounting between the United States and Mexico and news had reached Santa Fe from the capital in Mexico City that warned of the necessity to begin preparations for war between the two nations. Despite the tensions and fears that such news undoubtedly brought, when we look beyond the rhetoric of politicians, we find that life went on. It was spring and preparations had to be made to clean the *acequias* and plow the fields for another season of planting; livestock had to be tended and after a hard winter, maybe even some plans made to enjoy life a little.

One seemingly insignificant document that illustrates how life went on during these difficult times is a formal contract for a horse race entered into by the Pino family of Santa Fe and Francisco Tomás Cabesa de Baca of Peña Blanca. The document, dated March 18, 1846, was prepared by Trinidad Barcelo, second constitutional *alcalde* of the Santa Fe *ayuntamiento* (municipal council) and is found in the 1846 Judicial Proceedings of the *Mexican Archives of New Mexico*. The following is my translation of the contract.

> In the city of Santa Fe, capital of the Department of New Mexico, on the 18th of March of 1846, before me the citizen Trinidad Barcelo, 2nd constitutional alcalde and my assisting witnesses with whom I am acting as delegated judges due to the lack of public scribes (of whom there are none in the ter-

ritory), appeared personally the citizens Justo Pastor Pino and Miguel E. Pino of this city, whom I certify that I know personally as free men and gentleman of means, and these say:

The later of whom I named, with authorization from the citizen Francisco Tomás Cabesa de Baca of Peña Blanca, has contracted with the first named and he with the other, a horse race, that they state is to take place the upcoming Sunday from nine to eleven of the day, for the distance of 500 Castilian *varas*, on firm and level ground and expressed that the site of the designated race [is to be] on the plain (*el llano*) of the wagon road that runs near [or by] the house of the late Don Salvador Martín towards los Alamitos;

And that the horses in the race are the black (*prieto*) belonging to Justo Pastor Pino with the red (*colorado*) named "*mala ralla*" of Don Francisco Tomás Cabesa de Baca and that the wager is ten bred heifers, new and without lesions, to be turned over by the one that loses to the winner by the first day of May of the current year, to which they agree, as well as 206 yards of cloth to be turned over to the winner by the loser at the end of the race; that the riders shall be of equal weight and only if either of the horses falls ill or other legal contingency, from today to the hour of the race, shall justify cancellation of the race; if none of these apply, the one who does not run shall be responsible for the value of the contract as if the race had been run.

To assure all is valid and secure, it is stipulated in the present document to the national justices that recognize the legality of the present business, and principally those of this city so they may compel compliance before competent authority without appeal.

As such the gentlemen Justo Pastor Pino and Miguel Estanislado Pino certify before me, and they ask that in order to properly validate the present security I authorize the same, so I the referred to Alcalde (as the parties ask), say that I so authorize with the faculties with which I am conferred, signing it with the parties and assisting witnesses with whom I certify, on this 18th day of March of 1846.

Signed:

Trinidad Barcelo As assistants: Manuel Baca y Delgado
Justo Pastor Pino Calletano Garcia
Miguel E. Pino

The historical record does not tell us if the race was ever held. If the race was held, however, it would have been a greatly anticipated and well attended event. Horses have long been valued commodities in New Mexico and anyone who boasted of blood lines or the speed of his horse would certainly have been challenged by another who was certain that his horse had superior breeding and was faster.

It is unfortunate that we do not know if the race was held and who won. Imagine all the side bets that would have been made on the home town favorite and the heated discussions about the various attributes of each horse. One can visualize the cheering and exhortations of the crowd that lined the raceway and the inevitable disputes sparked by a close finish or the arguments about fair starts or violations of some unwritten rules. One cannot help but wish we had been there to witness this small but wonderful moment in our past that showed how life went on, despite the mounting tensions between the nascent Mexican Republic and its aggressive neighbor to the north.

The Orderly Succession to Office

One of the fascinating elements of how governments functioned during the Spanish and Mexican periods is how one governor assumed office from another when a new governor was appointed. It may be surprising to some that these successions were typically carried out in a very formal and orderly manner. This process is nowhere better documented than the surviving records of the late Mexican period.

During most of New Mexico's Mexican period (1821-1846) there was no office of lieutenant governor although someone with that title at times is listed as the senior government official in El Paso del Norte. Succession to the duties of office in the event of a governor's death or illness fell to the *primer vocal*, the most senior member of the *diputación* or Department Assembly. When the governor left the capitol in Santa Fe on official or personal business even for a few days, he had to notify the Assembly and formally turn over civil authority to the individual that held that position.

Documentation of the process of succession for a governor that was leaving office unfolds beautifully in the weeks following Governor Manuel Armijo's resignation from office on December 10, 1843. A month later, on January 9, 1844, Armijo, citing reasons of health, and apparently unwilling or unable to continue in office until his replacement was named, notified the Department Assembly that he was leaving. Two weeks later, Mariano Chaves y Castillo assumed "*mando del gobierno*," or command of the government, and was sworn in as interim governor at the Palace of the Governors.

Within a few days, the assembly prepared and sent the central government in Mexico a list of five nominees for the governorship. The full list is not in our archives, but indications are Mariano Martínez was at the top of the list. On February 12, 1844, Martínez wrote to the assembly, advising them he had heard (there must have been "leaks" *mas antes* too) that his name had been placed at the top of the list of nominees for governor. He thanked the assembly for the honor and assured them that if appointed he would do his best to serve the territory.

Over the next month, the nominations made their way through the Mexican hierarchy and on or about March 30, 1844, the decision was made to appoint Mariano Martínez as governor of New Mexico. The decision was immediately forwarded to the *Ministerio de Guerra y Marina* in Mexico City, where the appointment was confirmed and Martínez notified in a letter dated April 5, 1844.

Meanwhile, back in New Mexico, interim governor Mariano Chaves y Castillo became ill and informed the Assembly that he could no longer serve in the office. On April 12, unaware that the decision to appoint Martínez had already been made by the government in Mexico, the Assembly asked Manuel Armijo to return to Santa Fe and resume command of the government until his replacement was named. Armijo's response is not on record, but he must have refused the honor because Felipe Sena, as the most senior *vocal,* assumed the functions of governor that same day.

News of Mariano Martínez' appointment as governor arrived in Santa Fe on April 29, 1844. That day the Assembly and Martínez simultaneously advised each other that they had received notice of the appointment and after some discussion, set May 15 as the date for his inauguration to office. Martínez served as governor almost exactly one year. The correspondence logs for his term of office are a wonderful source of information for anyone wishing to refute the long held and erroneous notion that New Mexico was isolated, cut off from the government in Mexico and the world in general. His records show a regular, if not constant flow of correspondence from all parts of Mexico. Letters and printed broadsides from officials in Yucatán, Chiapas, Tamaulipas, Sinalóa, San Luis Potosí, Nuevo Leon, Morelia, Aguas Calientes, Puebla, Guanajuato, Zacatecas, Durango and Chihuahua kept New Mexico informed of local events, changes in government, and appointments to office. Newly appointed governors in New Mexico often received letters of congratulations and well- wishes from distant Mexican states and cities, indicating that news of what was happening in New Mexico was widely distributed to other parts of the Mexican Republic.

On April 14, 1845, Governor Martínez received orders from superior government in Mexico that he was to turn over the civil government to the "*vocal aquien corresponda,*" the Assembly member to whom it corresponds, and two weeks later, Martínez formally turned over the office to José Chaves as interim governor. By May 13, 1845, the Assembly had met, debated and prepared a "*Quintero de Gobernador,*" a list of five nominees for the central government in Mexico to consider as the next governor. The nominees, in the order of their listing, were Manuel Armijo, Mariano Chaves y Castillo (who died on May 17), Juan Perea, Antonio Ortiz, and Vicente Martínez. When Manuel Armijo was notified in late July 1845 that he had been selected for his third term as governor, little did he realize that he was also to be the last individual to succeed to the office of governor in New Mexico under Mexican rule.

Concerning Apache Captives

Among the many fascinating aspects of colonial history in New Mexico is the often violent and contentious relationship between the pueblos and Spanish and the nomadic tribes that surrounded the province. Among the many wonderful documents in our own Spanish Archives of New Mexico that tell us about these relationships is one dated in 1714. In this wonderfully preserved manuscript, Governor Juan Ignacio Flores Mogollón tells of the capture and disposition of two men, three women, and two children of the Faraone Apache. On August 18, 1714, Sebastián de Vargas, the *alcalde mayor* of the Pueblo of Pecos, appeared before Governor Flores Mogollón with the seven captives in custody. After Agustín, a Pecos Indian who "understood the Apache language and was fluent in the Castilian language," was sworn as interpreter, the captives were interrogated about their business at the pueblo.

In such proceedings, the witnesses were all sworn "in the name of our Lord God and the sign of the cross, under whose charge they promised to tell the truth." The captives, including the children, were individually questioned and asked where they had come from and what they were doing at the Pueblo of Pecos. It is difficult to determine what their real purpose was. Some indicated they had come on orders of their chief to see if the pueblo wanted to conduct some trade. But the inconsistencies in their testimony led the interrogators to conclude they were probably spying for a larger group that intended to raid the pueblo.

During the proceedings, a Pecos Indian named Uta testified the Faraones had killed his brother several years earlier during the administration of Governor Francisco Cubero (1697-1703). He also indicated the Faraones regularly came down from the Sandia Mountains to "steal horses and livestock from the pueblos of Galisteo, the said Pueblo of Pecos, and those of Santo Domingo, Bernalillo and the surrounding ranches." They also emphasized the Faraones frequently came to the settlements on the pretext of peaceful trade, but used the occasion to spy and plan their robberies. Indications are the residents of Pecos had determined to kill these captives outright but were prevented from doing so by the *alcalde mayor*. When Pecos Pueblo Governor Lorenzo Chistoe was asked why they wanted to kill the Faraones, he responded that the two captive adult men "were grand thieves" personally responsible for a majority of the thefts reported in the region.

On August 23, 1714, Governor Flores Mogollón ruled that Faraones were notorious and well-known thieves and concluded they had killed Uta's brother several years before. The wording of the document makes it difficult to determine if the evidence pointed directly to the captives or the Faraones in general, but it is clear that these seven individuals were destined to pay for the actions of their fellow tribesmen. The governor, continued:

> ...the declarations of the Indians of Pecos agree that all Faraones are public thieves and that these two had killed a Indian from said pueblo and that every hour of the day they carry out robberies in distinct parts of the kingdom, stealing horses and livestock, obliging me on many occasions to send out armed parties in pursuit. For their punishment...I order that the two adult Indians be taken to the mines where they are to be held with shackles so that they do not flee and continue their robberies and murders. The old woman, by reason of her advanced age, is to be... turned over to a citizen (*vecino*) of [Santa Cruz] de la Cañada...The two other women and two boys I order sold and sent to Sonora or other places where those that keep them can indoctrinate them and see if they can be brought into Our Holy Faith. From the [proceeds of their sale] I apply fifty pesos in charity to the Third Order of Saint Francis in Santa Fe and twenty five for my Secretary; from the remainder, the Alcalde Mayor of Pecos, Captain Sebastián de Vargas, may have fifty pesos for their capture and

having brought them from that jurisdiction to this villa.

As soon as Governor Flores Mogollón pronounced the sentences, Captain Alfonso (Alonso?) Real de Aguilar stepped forward and offered to purchase the two women and children for 200 pesos. The governor immediately agreed to the proposition and ordered the captives be turned over to Real de Aguilar and the two hundred pesos distributed as per his order.

The story of these captives ends here. The document does not specify when and if the two men were shipped off to Sonora or if Real de Aguilar took the women and children out of New Mexico. Later documents show a shipment of Apache captives to northern Mexico but there is no way to determine if these seven were part of those transactions. Who knows? Maybe the women and children lived out their lives as *captivos* (captive servants) in the Real de Aguilar household and their descendants are now part of that marvelous genetic mix that makes modern New Mexico.

Resettlement of the Rio Abajo

We often forget or do not realize how difficult and dangerous life on the frontier could be *mas antes*. One of the best examples of these dangers is in the great difficulty with which the *rio abajo* was resettled following the *reconquista* of 1692-93. It was the 1740s before the *genízaro* settlements of Valencia and Cerro de Tomé extended the frontier a few miles south of the *villa* of Alburquerque. It took another half century for settlement to move south beyond Belen and by 1800 Sabinal was the southernmost community along the ancient *camino real* that connected New Mexico to the outside world.

On January 18, 1800 the Spanish government announced an ambitious program of frontier resettlement and ordered Governor Fernando Chacón that in compliance with the Royal Regulations for Presidios of 1772, he was to "...reestablish the ruined settlements of Senecú, Socorro, Alamillo and Sevilleta, situated on the royal road that goes from El Paso to Santa Fe."

The instructions were very specific. Socorro was to be re-established first and a squad of soldiers stationed there until the community was able to defend itself. The settlement grant was to consist of the customary four square leagues. Land for a church and house for a priest was to be set aside, and each settler assigned a lot on which to build his own home and cultivate, making sure enough land was left for other settlers that may come later. All the settlers were to be married and each was to transport their family to Socorro along with their tools, livestock, and weapons. Once Socorro was established, the governor was to "re-establish the other ruined settlements along the *camino real* as the opportunity arises." The governor was also ordered to scout other sites that might be suitable to establish an unbroken string of settlements every twenty to forty miles along the *camino real.*

Governor Chacón responded quickly. He revealed a plan to begin the process of resettlement at Alamillo because he felt that the jump from Sabinal to Socorro was too great to accomplish at this time. He pointed out that Socorro was located on the opposite bank (west side) of the river from the *camino real,* making access to it very difficult at certain times of the year and impossible to defend under the circumstances. He had also considered re-establishing the Puesto de Sevilleta first, being that it was closer to Sabinal, but recent flooding of the Rio del Norte (Rio Grande) had washed away all the old *acequias* and it would be too difficult and expensive to rebuild.

For these and other reasons, he had decided to begin the resettlement at Alamillo. To begin this process, he issued a *bando* (edict) enlisting "all the poor who do not own land or possess the means to work the land." But he received very little response and found it necessary to seize a number of "wanderers, servants, gamblers, adulterers, and other incorrigibles" to start the resettlement. In all, the new settlement consisted of sixty two families, a number of which had to be gathered by force. Chacón commented dryly that "one could not help but notice that the departure of these people was not without some commotion, particularly in the capital [Santa Fe], where it became necessary for the troops to assist local officials."

According to Chacón's plan, these reluctant settlers were provided with oxen, tools, and enough food to last six or seven months until their own crops could be harvested. A squad consisting of one officer, one corporal, one *caravinero* and eighteen soldiers from the *presidio,* or garrison at Santa Fe, and twenty *vecinos* from *rio arriba* were assigned to provide escort and security. The troops were to be relieved every two months, and the *vecinos* every thirty days. These would be supported by troops stationed at the outpost at Sabinal if necessary. The settlers themselves were provided with twelve muskets and ammunition. Chacón admitted the resettlement project would prove expensive and implored the *comandante general* to approve the plans so its success might minimize the ever present threat of Indian raids and subsequent abandonment that comes from the "natural fear of the women and children."

Chacón's report includes a chart listing the oxen, tools and supplies provided the reluctant *pobladores* (settlers) of Alamillo. Aside from the oxen and weapons, the list includes twelve axes, twelve adze, twelve shovels, eighteen hoes, and twenty four hides for making hinges and buckets. They were also provided 400 fanegas (a colonial measure of approximately two-and a half bushels) of corn to tide them over until harvest.

The archives do not tell us how long the settlement at Alamillo held out. Their life had to have been difficult – notwithstanding that many, if not most of them, had been relocated against their will. It is clear, however, that the Spanish government's ambitious hopes for a string of settlements along the camino real to El Paso del Norte soon stalled. Socorro, for example, was not re-established permanently until about 1815, when seventy families settled on the site of the old pueblo.

Campaign Regulations of 1791

On November 21, 1791, Pedro de Nava, the *comandante general* of the *Provincias Internas,* a political jurisdiction that included New Mexico, issued a set of detailed instructions from his headquarters in Chihuahua. These instructions were to serve as basic regulations for all commanders that led campaigns against enemy tribes. They are several pages in length and too detailed to duplicate in their entirely here, but the following summary shows the manner in which Nava expected expeditions be organized and led.

Nava expected every commander of a campaign to have a "perfect knowledge" of the frontier. Failing that, they were to assure they had the services of experienced and competent subordinates and informants who could assist in areas where he was not familiar with the terrain. Field commanders were also to assure that the livestock and equipment of his men were frequently inspected and in a proper state of readiness.

A commander was to manage these scouts and spies, regardless whether they were Indians or *vecinos,* with "skill and intuition" and should not ignore advice they might offer. When preparing an attack or arranging a retreat, he needed to make sure his men were well prepared and dispersed. Commanders were also reminded that despite all possible precautions, they also needed to take luck into account and be prepared to react to unforeseen circumstances firmly and with flexibility. Commanders were reminded that distinguished actions built a soldier's reputation and helped his career.

If a commander received reports of Indians raids three or four days after they occurred, he was to consider whether too much time had passed for an effective pursuit. If a detachment was sent to pursue raiders, it was to be in proportion to the number of enemy reported and for the period necessary to accomplish the mission. Prudent commanders also equipped an expedition for a few extra days in case of unforeseen circumstances.

The most certain and best method of finding the enemy was to follow the trail or tracks they left behind. They were cautioned not to cross a plain located between two mountains during daylight because an expedition could be observed from the distant heights. Trails were to be followed in a roundabout manner, leaving the trail and returning to it at some point when the other mountain was reached. When a trail crossed a plain that could not be observed from a mountain, the troops were to proceed in a dispersed formation in order to minimize the dust they raised. When an expedition was in danger of being observed, they were to halt while scouts went ahead by day, then the bulk of the force could advance at night and join the spies at a designated point.

When a fresh trail was spotted that denoted a nearby enemy encampment, the commander was to hide his men or approach in such a manner that they could not be discovered. He was to review the situation personally or with his scouts to determine the best means of launching a surprise attack. Care was to be taken to cover approaches to the enemy camp and some of his best men stationed on high ground to cover the enemy's escape routes. After he made sure their supplies and equipment were secured, troops could advance on foot, firing on their objective as they did. Squads mounted on horseback could then use their lances to follow up the surprise attack. The commander was to consider that if he attacked at a time of day when the sun is low along the horizon, his troops needed to advance from the direction that allowed them to avoid the glare of the sun. If circumstances required him to retreat, he was to proceed over the most advantageous route that assured the safety of his men. Half to one third of the men were to lay down cover fire in alternating groups in order to effectively protect the withdrawal.

Subsequent paragraphs remind commanders they were required to keep a campaign diary that detailed their operations and results of the campaign. This diary was to include a list of livestock or other spoils taken from the enemy. Branded livestock was to be turned over to owners but unbranded livestock could be distributed equally among the members of the expedition. Captured bows, arrows, quivers, and tanned hides were to be divided equally among any allied Indians that accompanied the expedition. Finally, captives recovered from the Indians were to be identified and turned over to their parents. Those that could not be identified were to be sent to Nava in Chihuahua for his personal disposition.

Nava concluded his instructions by assuring his commanders in the field that he would not usurp any credit for successful campaigns or any distinguished actions they carried out. He assured them that commanders of such expeditions would be "especially recognized so they can be rewarded."

The Mission Census of 1808

Figuring the population of New Mexico at any particular point of the colonial period has always been a tricky proposition. There were numerous official census taken during the colonial period as well as a number of "mission census" done by the Franciscan Friars of the Custody of the Conversion of Saint Paul that was responsible for the Pueblo missions and towns of Spanish period New Mexico. One can wonder how complete these are, but all of them can teach us something. One of the interesting mission census found in the New Mexico's colonial-era archives commonly known as the Land Record of New Mexico was submitted by Fr. Josef Benito Pereyro on December 31, 1808. The opening paragraph of the census describes its purpose and scope: "Notice of the missions occupied by the [Franciscans]...of the ministers, stipends, and number of souls of both sexes in the ...Province of New Mexico at the end of December 1808."

The census then lists the missions and *villas* of the province, with the population enumerated by sex in separate columns for the Indians of the missions and the "Españoles y Castas (Spanish and castes)."

	Indios	**Españoles y Castas**
Villa Capital de Santa Fe		4,734
N.S. de los Angeles de Pecos	132	646
San Diego de Tesuque	156	212
San Francisco de Nambe	186	38
N.S. de Guadalupe de Pojoaque	83	220
Villa de la Cañada		2,315

San Juan de los Cavalleros	201	1,733
San Lorenzo de Picuris	309	626
San Geronimo de Taos	527	1,255
Santo Tomas de Abiquiú	122	1,816
Santa Clara	213	1,094
San Yldefonso	272	270
Santo Domingo	701	469
San Buenaventura de Cochití	672	593
San Philipe	394	359
Santa Ana	535	96
N.S. de la Asunción de Zia	278	
San Diego de Xemes	285	465
San Josef de la Laguna	1,007	299
San Esteban de Acoma	797	
N.S. de Guadalupe de Zuñi	1,557	11
N. S. de Belen	135	1,982
San Agustín de la Ysleta	471	581
Villa de Alburquerque		4,051
N. S. de los Dolores de Sandia	358	227
Totals	10,063	24,682

The total population of the twenty two pueblo missions (the nineteen of today plus Pecos, Abiquiú and Belen – Pecos had not yet been abandoned, and the later two *genízaro* settlements were still officially considered pueblos) and three Spanish *villas* in New Mexico was listed at 34,745, and would have included the numerous towns within the villa's particular jurisdiction. A total of seventeen Friars served the entire province. Compared to the 33,326 population referred to in this document for the previous, 1806 mission census, the population had increased by 1,419 individuals, or approximately four percent.

In addition to the raw population figures, Fray Josef includes footnotes for each of the listed missions and villas. His notes for Santa Fe, for example, tell us that the position of parish priest was vacant and being served by the *presidio* chaplain, Fr. Francisco de Hosio. He also notes that the parish church itself was rebuilt by the late don Antonio Ortiz and other devotees, but principally at the personal expense of don Antonio.

As he goes down the list, Fr. Josef notes the condition of each church building, comments on the type and condition of vestments and church vessels. At Tesuque, for example, he tells us that the church and convent are in good condition but is lacking white vestments; the church at Santa Cruz de la Cañada was in reasonable condition, and that it had been re-roofed in1783; at Picuris, a new missal had been purchased at the cost of thirty pesos; Santa Clara had adequate vestments and sacred vessels, but the church walls had a number of cracks in need of repair; and San Josef de la Laguna was in good condition and had all the ornamentation and vessels it needed, as well as an iron utensil used to make hosts. The Belen mission was also singled out for praise. Built in 1793, Fr. Josef indicated that José Pino and his neighbors had supplied the church with all the ornamentation and vessels needed and the *convento*, or priest's residence, was "the best in all the custody."

On a more secular note, Fr. Josef pointed out that of all the pueblos, those of Laguna, Acoma and Zuñi were the most industrious. These, like the others, cultivated their lands and hunted buffalo and deer, but also made "*mantas, cotones and tilmas*" for their own use and for trade with the other pueblos and Españoles. He also pointed out the Spanish citizens wove vast quantities of cotton and woolen cloth and produced many hides and pelts from the buffalo and deer they hunted. He praised both the *vecinos*, or Spanish citizens and Pueblos for the endless scout and campaign duty they carried out at their own expense.

El Tambor, the Military Drummer

The *tambor*, or drummer, holds a special place in the military and civic affairs of colonial Spain. While we generally visualize a drummer marching valiantly at the front of a file of solders advancing into battle, drummers also served as a rallying point and played a critical role in communicating orders on a chaotic battlefield. In civil affairs, the drummer also called citizens together for important public announcements.

So it was in New Mexico, where the drummer is mentioned in a broad variety of documents in the Spanish and Mexican Archives of New Mexico. The earliest if these quite often cite Esteban Rodríguez, who served for several decades as the *tambor* for the *presidio* (military garrison) company of Santa Fe and public crier for civil affairs. One of the earliest of these documents recalls the publication, or public reading, of a *bando* (official decree) issued by Governor Juan Ignacio Flores Mogollón in 1714. It noted the publication was accomplished "with the playing of the military instruments in the customary places by the voice of Esteban Rodríguez, drummer…"

More than four decades later, Rodríquez' skill was still being touted by his commanding officers and peers. In 1757 the officers and men of the Santa Fe *presidio* noted that upon Rodríguez impending retirement no one else apparently knew how to play the drum properly. They asked the governor to order Rodríguez to return to service and if necessary, compel him to teach another to play the instrument. The petition emphasized the importance of this "martial instrument" to instill courage in troops and strike fear in an enemy. Governor Francisco Antonio Marín del Valle agreed. He ordered Rodríguez be assigned the next vacancy that occurred in the *presidio* ranks so that he could provide daily instruction to the person of his choosing. He was to continue until that person learned to "play the drum well" and take over the position when needed. At this time, the term *tambor* referred to the drummer and not necessarily the instrument itself. The drum itself was usually referred to as the *caja*, quite literally, a "box." A typical entry would note the sounding of the drum as "*a son de la caja*."

A careful review of enlistment papers and musters of the Spanish and Mexican period documents reveals the names of individuals who held the position of *tambor* throughout the nearly one and half centuries for which the Santa Fe *presidio* is documented. A cursory review of these documents shows, for example, Josef Prada's enlistment as *tambor* in 1778 at thirteen years of age as well as the subsequent service of Juan Varela in the position until he was replaced by José Alarí. Financial records of the *presidio* also show the salaries paid to the troops throughout this period. While the salary of the typical *soldado*, or lowest ranking enlisted man, was 240 pesos a year, the *tambor* was slightly more than half that amount. The *presidio* salary accounts for 1796 show the tambor was budgeted at 144 pesos a year, or twelve pesos a month.

While the tambor was literally at the lowest rung of the military totem pole, they could look forward to climbing the ranks. A royal order issued in 1797 noted that Manuel Malo, who held the rank of sergeant, had served as a drummer for thirty four years and consequently, qualified for a pension at retirement. This seems to indicate that not all drummers stayed at the critical, but lowly position and salary indicated by the official tables of organization. They could be promoted to higher rank (and salary) while retaining the tasks of *tambor* when circumstances called for it.

On the other hand, most drummers who moved up the ranks did not retain the status of *tambor*, but rather assumed higher ranks as vacancies occurred. In 1797, for example, Governor Fernando Chacón reported that he found it necessary to find and teach an unnamed young man "of good qualities" in order to place him in the position of *tambor* when another individual assumed the higher rank of *soldado*. Chacón's report does not mention the names of these two individuals but the timing is such it may have referred to the retirement of Manual Malo, mentioned above.

The problems associated with finding qualified individuals to learn the critical skills of an effective drummer are also noted in a number of Mexican-period documents. In 1830, Governor José Antonio Chaves informed the *comandante general* in Chihuahua that the drummer of the Santa Fe *presidio* knew only a few very old tunes. Consequently, he sent Ramón Martínez with an escort of two soldiers to Chihuahua so he could learn more from the drummer at that *presidio.* The records do not indicate how long Martinez stayed in Chihuahua and whether he returned to New Mexico with a wider repertoire of tunes.

The position of *tambor* was replaced with the *clarín*, or bugler, during the late Mexican period. However, the image of these individuals, many of them little more than boys, furiously beating the drum to rally troops in battle or call together a crowd to hear the latest public announcement, will be forever vivid in our minds.

San Miguel del Bado – Defending the Eastern Frontier

New Mexico's frontiers were vast and forbidding places in the eighteenth century. The Taos region was settled permanently (but not extensively) by the early 1700s and Santa Rosa de Lima and Santo Tomás Apostol de Abiquiú were established along the northwest frontier by the 1750s. In eastern New Mexico, settlements spread along the Rio Pecos but did not venture far from the parent communities south of Pecos until early in the nineteenth century. Through much of this period San Miguel del Bado (historically, the name was usually spelled with a "B" although it is usually spelled Vado today) was the principal settlement along this easternmost frontier.

The basic difficulties of life on the frontier were made more so by the dangers settlers faced from the various Indian tribes that regularly raided their flocks, stole livestock, killed settlers, and kidnapped women and children. These problems eventually led to a decision by the Mexican government to establish a permanent *destacamento*, or military outpost, at San Miguel to help protect the settlements there.

The practice of stationing *presidio* soldiers at San Miguel del Bado (so designated because of the *bado*, or crossing, of the Pecos River) on a long-term basis began as early as November 1826, when the *cabo* (a rank roughly equivalent to a corporal) José Larrañaga and nine soldiers were ordered to proceeded there and stay "until the receipt of new orders." There is no indication how long Larrañaga and his men stayed but troops continued to be stationed at San Miguel through the 1830s in response to numerous reports of Indian raids in the region and because San Miguel served as a depot, or receiving point for the American caravans that made their way to New Mexico over the Santa Fe Trail. In late March of 1830, José Antonio Vizcarra, as *comandante principal*, or military commander of the Santa Fe *presidio*, dispatched the *alférez* José Silva and twenty- seven men to San Miguel to establish an outpost at that location. Silva and his men departed from Santa Fe on March 29, 1830, marched through Apache Canyon past Pecos to the settlement at El Gusano, and arrived at San Miguel del Bado on March 31.

Silva's report shows they remained at San Miguel for three days "*sin novedad*," or with nothing significant to report. One can presume they spent this time unpacking their gear and setting up camp. On April 4, Silva began sending out scouting parties of nine men to search for locations where hostile raiding parties could hide and approach the communities without being spotted. The scouting parties rotated this duty every third day. On April 10, Silva received word from the local *alcalde* that seven men had been killed by Indians at a sheep camp near the *ancón de Felipe Sanches*. Silva immediately sent a messenger to Santa Fe to report the incident and prepared to pursue the raiders and recover the bodies.

Silva, fifteen soldiers and ten militiamen from San Miguel left the settlement on April 11 and reached Anton Chico that evening where they encamped for the night. The following morning they proceeded to Agua Negra which they reached on the 13th before arriving at the *ancón de Felipe Sanches*. Silva and his patrol spent two days scouting the area in search of the bodies reportedly killed by raiding Indians. However, they found only one body and concluded the report had been vastly exaggerated. Unable to do more, the troops returned to San Miguel on afternoon of the 14th, arriving at their camp at three o'clock the afternoon of the 16th.

For the next two weeks, Silva and his men settled into a camp routine of drill, inspections, and the rotating scouts that went out every third day. Silva remained with his men at San Miguel until April 31, when he received orders to turn over command of the *destacamento* to his unnamed *cabo* (corporal) and return to Santa Fe.

This troop presence at San Miguel apparently had a positive effect on hostilities in the region as raids seem to have subsided during the subsequent weeks. However, raiding resumed towards the end of summer and a series of reports noted that the Pawnee had attacked Anton Chico in late August 1830 and killed one citizen. A troop of forty two men pursued the raiders to the Rio Colorado but were unable to catch them. Subsequent raids prompted Governor José Antonio Chaves to recommend to his superiors in Chihuahua that a permanent outpost of thirty men be established at San Miguel to help protect the eastern frontier.

I have found no record that shows when this permanent outpost was officially established at San Miguel. By September 1832, however, solders were stationed there on at least a semi-permanent basis and correspondence and reports of the period begin to refer to families of the soldiers being there. Certainly, by November of 1832, correspondence of *comandante principal* José Antonio Vizcarra mentions official recruiting for the company at San Miguel del Bado. From 1832 until the U. S. occupation in 1846, a company that numbered between twenty and thirty men and officers was stationed at San Miguel – making this community a key element in the tenuous defense of New Mexico's eastern frontier.

Part Two: The People, Places and Events of Territorial New Mexico, 1846-1912

New Mexico's Loyalties Questioned During the Spanish American War

New Mexico was long been associated with the Spanish American War of 1898, principally because of the men recruited from New Mexico and Arizona to serve with Teddy Roosevelt's "Rough Riders." This association was cemented forever during the years following the war by the Rough Rider Re-unions held at Las Vegas and the museum of that name still maintained there in memory of this brave group of westerners. However, there are other elements of this conflict related to New Mexico that deserve attention, namely the questions that arose at the time about whether New Mexicans would remain loyal to their ancient Spanish fatherland or to the United States of America.

Officially, New Mexicans seemed to support Cuba's efforts to gain its independence from Spain. "I am heartily in favor of intervention in behalf of Cuba," wrote Governor Miguel A. Otero on March 23, 1898, in response to an inquiry from *The New York World.* Otero also expressed his opinion that the people of New Mexico supported the cabinet's call for direct intervention following the February 15, 1898 sinking of the American battleship *Maine* in Havana harbor.

Governor Otero even wrote to the Secretary of War and confidently offered "a full regiment of cavalry - ninety five per cent Spanish speaking," if and when hostilities should break out between Spain and the United States. "It occurs to me," wrote Otero, "that our volunteers would be very desirable in a Spanish speaking country." As it turns out, Governor Otero was overly optimistic about how many Spanish speaking New Mexicans would actually volunteer for service in the upcoming war, but that is another story.

The issue of New Mexicans' loyalties surfaced as soon as war was declared with Spain on April 25, 1898. The following day, the *Santa Fe New Mexican* published a story about rumors that prominent New Mexicans had sent telegrams to government officials in Washington warning that the native peoples of New Mexico were openly sympathetic to Spain and that troops should be sent here "to avoid an open revolt." The newspaper vehemently denied that such as sentiment existed in the territory and noted that New Mexico's native peoples had "repeatedly proved their loyalty to the American flag."

Over the next several days a number of patriotic rallies were held throughout the territory. At one held the evening of April 26 in Santa Fe, Governor Otero delivered a rousing speech which repudiated the rumors of disloyalty and emphasized his own feelings on the issue:

> I am a New Mexican, and in saying that I am saying that I am an American...We have a war on our hands now, and we want no Republicans, no Democrats, no Populists, in fact no politics to interfere with its successful prosecution. Let us all be Americans.

Other speeches followed. The crowd enthusiastically endorsed a resolution denouncing the "designing and evil-minded persons [who] have circulated malicious statements to the effect that the Spanish people of New Mexico are giving their loyalty to the Spanish government in the present war with the United States." The rally built to a rousing close when the band struck up the "Star Spangled Banner" and three cheers for "Cuba Libre" were raised.

The question of loyalty remained subdued for a few weeks until more rumors surfaced in June. This time, it was alleged that the Spanish flag had been flown over the church at Santa Cruz and had been used during processions held there on the feast of the Holy Cross on May 3 and at the feast of Corpus Christi a few weeks later. The rumors were persistent enough to prompt the Reverend John Roux, pastor at Santa Cruz, to write a letter to Governor Otero protesting the "terrible and calumnious talk about the people of Santa Cruz." He denied they had a Spanish flag at Santa Cruz and insisted that no such flag had ever flown over the church. "The only flag ...

[that] will float over the Church of Santa Cruz will be the American flag for the 4th of July. Here at Santa Cruz," he concluded, "the pastor and the people are true Americans."

While it has not been possible to confirm the source of these rumors, Father Roux felt the ones related to Santa Cruz had originated from one unnamed individual who had been sent to Española to recruit volunteers for the contingent of New Mexicans being organized for the war. According to Father Roux, that individual was known to Governor Otero, but his name remained out of print. Due in part to the malicious efforts of mysterious individuals such as this, it would take two future world wars to prove the loyalty and patriotism of native New Mexicans.

Lost Documents Returned to New Mexico

Few states in the Union can claim to possess a documentary heritage equal to that which New Mexico has in its Spanish and Mexican archival collections. However, one cannot help but wonder how much more complete these documentary treasures could be if over the years, so many government officials and private citizens had not taken advantage of the casual, if not indifferent, care in which the ancient Spanish and Mexican documents were kept in the nineteenth century, and pilfered hundreds if not thousands of documents for their personal use.

Some of these "lost" documents are known to have survived because individuals who took them, or their heirs, sold or donated them to collectors and archival repositories outside New Mexico. One of the best examples of these "fugitive records," as they are sometimes known, are found in the William G. Ritch collection now held at the Huntington Library in California. Ritch held several positions in New Mexico's territorial government, including several terms as Territorial Secretary between 1873 and 1882. In this position he was the official custodian and guardian of all of New Mexico's government records. Ritch also had a keen interest in New Mexico history and is credited with the publication of our first *Blue Book* in 1882. However, in the course of his research into New Mexico's past, he also selectively removed hundreds of documents from the archives and retained them in his personal possession after he left public office. These documents were later sold to the aforementioned library.

Although the Ritch Collection is one of the more prominent examples of how a portion of our documentary heritage has ended up in other states, the sad truth is that others contributed to this loss. Many officials appointed to serve in New Mexico's territorial government were from other states. When their term of office ended, many simply packed up their records and took them back home with their other possessions. Enough documentation exists of surprised incumbents noting they found their office bereft of records to conclude that this was fairly common practice. Consequently, a significant number of New Mexico's archives have ended up in places other than where they belong, the New Mexico State Records Center and Archives in Santa Fe.

Occasionally, however, we hear of "lost" documents which found their way back to the archives. One such story begins with a letter received by Governor Octaviano Larrazolo from Mr. Agustine E. Bourgine of Yountville, California in May, 1919. Mr. Bourgine notified Governor Larrazolo of an article he had seen in a Washington state newspaper which described two Spanish era documents that had been offered to the Eastern Washington (State) Historical Society by a Captain John Grey of Spokane.

On May 22, 1919, Larrazolo acknowledged the letter, thanked Bourgine for the information and assured him that he would take immediate steps to recover the documents for the archives in New Mexico. That same day, Larrazolo fired off a letter to Captain Grey about the documents and asked Grey to consider returning the documents to New Mexico. Larrazolo had somehow learned that the documents in question had been "entrusted" to Grey by prominent attorneys and political figures Stephen B. Elkins and Thomas B. Catron, more than thirty years earlier. "As an act of justice," wrote Larrazolo, "these documents should be returned to New Mexico...I have no doubt that you realize how unfair it would be to have those ancient documents, that properly belong to this state, placed in the archives of another state..."

In the meantime, Governor Larrazolo contacted Catron, who confirmed that he "or the late Senator Elkins" had left the documents with Grey "for safekeeping." Carton offered no explanation how he and Elkins had come into possession of the documents in the first place or what need they had of "safekeeping," but at Governor Larrazolo's request, Catron wrote to Grey and suggested the documents be returned to New Mexico.

Captain Grey immediately sent the documents to Governor Larrazolo by registered mail. By June 18, less than a month after they had been initially requested, two significant documents from New Mexico's Spanish era - one a

1698 manuscript by Pedro Rodriguez Cubero regarding several aspects of the re-colonization of New Mexico, the other, a 1742 report of an official *visita*, or inspection of the province by Governor Gaspar Domingo de Mendoza, were back where they belonged - in the same archives at the Palace of the Governors from which they had probably been taken in the first place.

As a consequence of an odd but propitious series of events, the story of these two "lost" documents had a happy ending. These two valuable and interesting manuscripts were once again (and still are) part of the official Spanish Archives of New Mexico, available to anyone interested in adding to their knowledge of New Mexico history.

The Errant Government Safe

Among the many seemingly unimportant but nonetheless interesting stories of our past is one which begins with allegations of misuse of government property involving, of all things, an iron safe. The story of this errant safe begins with a letter dated October 3, 1885, from Charles E. Coon, Assistant Secretary of Interior, to Jonathon S. Miller, the Commissioner of Internal Revenue at the United States Treasury Department. Coon informed Miller that he had received information that the Collector of Internal Revenue in Santa Fe, Silas W. Fisher, had loaned a government safe to an unnamed individual. In Coon's view, such unauthorized use of government property was bad enough, but making matters worse, and possibly why officials at this level of government were involved in a seemingly trivial matter, was that the safe was being used by that individual in a building which was "used for gambling!" Concerned about a possible controversy, Miller immediately wrote to Fisher and demanded a "full statement of the facts."

Fisher's report explained that he had in fact loaned a safe to a businessman named Henry Lewis. He indicated that an "American Steam Safe Co." iron safe had been shipped to Santa Fe from the Internal Revenue office at Tucson, Arizona, when the Arizona and New Mexico offices had been consolidated in 1883. Fisher indicated he has no use for the safe and because he had no space for it in the New Mexico office, he had allowed C. B. Heywood, publisher of the *Santa Fe New Mexican Review*, to use the safe in lieu of storage costs. When Heywood moved his office, he left the safe in the vacant building, and the building owner had informed Fisher that he would have to charge storage if it was left there.

Not wanting in incur unauthorized and unbudgeted expenses, Fisher arranged with Henry Lewis to move the safe to his place of business and to use it in lieu of storage costs. Fisher does not specify what kind of business Lewis conducted, but did say this consisted of a few "club rooms." Fisher felt this arrangement was not only proper, but saved the government $100 a year in storage expenses. He claimed that if he had done anything wrong, it was only because he was "too zealous" in carrying out his duties.

Federal officials finally concluded it was in the best interests of everyone involved to recover the safe from Lewis and offer it to another government office. By the end of November, Territorial Secretary George W. Lane had agreed that he could use the safe in his office and asked the Secretary of Interior to have Fisher deliver it to him. All seemed well and good, until Fischer requested reimbursement of twenty - five dollars in expenses he incurred to have the safe delivered to Secretary Lane. For several weeks, Lane and the Commissioner of Internal Revenue exchanged letters, each denying responsibility for the unexpected expense. There is no record of who ended up paying the bill.

Despite the controversy about moving expenses, it finally seemed the errant U. S. government safe had found a home in the office of the Territorial Secretary. But the safe came to public attention once again in 1889 when Benjamin M. Thomas replaced George W. Lane as Territorial Secretary. When Thomas entered his new position, he found the office completely devoid of files and records. When Thomas asked Lane about this, Lane informed him he had taken the records with him, claiming they were "his personal belongings." Lane also refused to provide Thomas with the combination of the safe. After several frustrating weeks, Thomas was forced to hire a locksmith to open the safe. Thomas does not report on what he found in the safe except for a cash box, but it too was locked and the key was nowhere to be found.

Following more frustrating attempts to see if Lane could produce the key, Thomas finally had a locksmith disassemble the lock on the cash box. In his letters on the subject, Thomas does not say what he found in the cash box, but did seem relieved to get past this "small, but rasping problem." At least he now had use of the safe.

But the safe continued to vex New Mexico's government officials. Late in 1889, Thomas sent the United States Treasury a bill for the expense of opening of the safe and repairing the lock on the cash box. The federal officials curtly responded that since this expense had been incurred through the neglect of Thomas' predecessor (Lane), they would not pay it. The record does not show how much the bill was, but Thomas did note later that it had been paid from territorial funds.

The safe disappears from the historical record after this latest incident. I had hoped the Office of Secretary of State had inherited it from its territorial predecessors, but it seems to have disappeared a long time ago. One wonders if it was damaged and subsequently discarded after the capitol burned in 1892. Or is it is possible that some state agency still has an old "American Steam Safe Company" safe in storage somewhere, wondering what to do with it? Maybe we should suggest they leave well enough alone before they breathe new life into the story of our errant "U. S. Government safe."

Letters Home

There are very few surviving examples of personal "letters from the front" in New Mexico's nineteenth century archives. Two rare exceptions are found among the miscellaneous letters and diaries at the State Records Center and Archives in Santa Fe. These letters were written by two men – probably an uncle and a nephew- who both happened to be stationed at Camp Plummer, an obscure military post established about two miles south of the northern New Mexico community of Los Ojos in late 1866. These two letters provide a rare and intimate look at what soldiers stationed along the New Mexican frontier wrote home about. In both cases, the letters refer to events that are substantiated by records of the military post itself.

Both letters were sent from Camp (or Fort) Plummer and addressed to don José Ygnacio Silva, possibly in Santa Fe. The first, addressed December 7, 1866 is from Carpio Silva, who addresses don José as "my very respected brother." The second, dated March 23, 1867, from José Dolores Silva, addresses don José as "my beloved and never forgotten father," hence the conclusion that Carpio and José Dolores were uncle and nephew (although José Dolores refers to Carpio as his brother).

Carpio and José Dolores Silva enlisted together in the Regiment of New Mexico Mounted Volunteers at Santa Fe on May 3, 1865. Both enlisted for three-year terms, Carpio as a sergeant and José Dolores as a corporal. Their rank at enlistment suggests they both had previous military experience. José Dolores was promoted to sergeant on November 1, 1866. The fact they both were able to read and write undoubtedly contributed to their rapid rise through the ranks.

The Silvas' posting at Camp Plummer began when Company "A," Battalion of New Mexico Volunteers, was ordered out of Fort Union on October 23, 1866. The unit proceeded to Tierra Amarilla, where they were to provide military protection to the settlements of that region. The seventy men and two commissioned officers of Company "A" arrived at their post in mid-November and quickly began construction of the buildings that constituted the military post named Camp Plummer. On November 29, the U. S. Army paymaster and his escort arrived at the post to pay the troops. Little more than a week later, Carpio wrote to don José, informing him he had sent one hundred dollars with the "priest from El Rito." The priest was planning to be in Santa Fe later that month, and would presumably deliver the money to don José. A postscript from José Dolores sent "greetings to my brother Juan José and little sister Doloritas and her family."

The "priest from El Rito" alluded to in Carpio's letter was the Rev. Pedro Bernal, who was actually the pastor at Santo Tomás Apostol in Abiquiú. This issue of the money they sent home and other news prompted José Dolores to write a second letter nearly four months later.

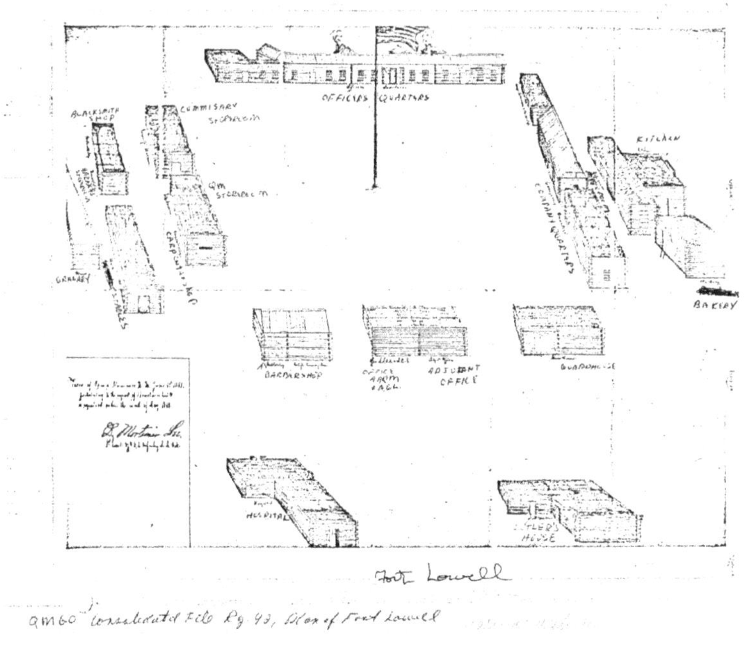

Layout of Camp Plummer/Fort Lowell, 1868. National Archives, Record Group 43, Plan of Fort Lowell

On March 23, 1867, José Dolores wrote to don José, informing him that Carpio and a detachment of soldiers had been sent to El Nacimiento. He also advised that a corporal from that detachment had recently arrived at the fort with news that Carpio was alive and well. Carpio's assignment is well-documented in Camp Plummer's military records. These show that on March 8, 1867, Sergeant Silva and ten enlisted men were ordered to proceed to Abiquiú and from there to the "head of the Rio Puerco." There, Silva and his men were to provide "protection [to] the parties that are to locate a settlement in that region, until they have themselves established securely in that place [.]" The settlement they were assigned to protect may have been the present-day community of Cuba in northern Sandoval County. Silva and his detachment were issued rations for sixty days, but they did not stay the full two months. Silva and his men returned to Camp Plummer on April 7.

José Dolores' letter also expressed worry about the one hundred dollars they sent the previous December with Padre Bernal. José Dolores was concerned that don José had not confirmed whether he had received the money. José Dolores asked his father to send word immediately by the courier that delivered his letter or by the next regular mail. José Dolores closed his letter with a fond salutation to his mother, recalling the many blessing she bestowed on him daily and his desire to see her very soon.

José Dolores had the opportunity to see his parents much sooner than expected. On October 5, 1867, a unit of the U. S. 37th Infantry replaced Company "A" of the New Mexico Volunteers and took over garrison duties at Camp Plummer. The following month, the Volunteers were mustered out of the service at Santa Fe. Carpio and José Dolores apparently joined their respective families and went back to civilian life. Their military experience, however, left us with a valuable "voice from the past" that provides us a brief glimpse of what soldiers wrote home about "*mas antes*."

Elisha V. Long, New Mexico's Romantic Judge

Judge Elisha V. Long. Boaz Long Collection #919. NM State Records Center and Archives.

Elisha Van Buren Long was one of territorial New Mexico's most distinguished jurists. He was appointed to the position of justice to the New Mexico Supreme Court early in the administration of Governor Edmund G. Ross (1885-1889) and served in that capacity for nearly a decade. In those days, the Supreme Court judges also served as District Court judges and traveled extensively through their respective circuits. During the course of his travels, Judge Long kept in touch with his wife and family through an intensive and often intimate correspondence. A wonderful collection of his professional and personal letters was maintained by his family and eventually deposited into the New Mexico State Records Center and Archives.

Judge Long's correspondence reveals much about his professional and personal life. Details of his travels, political concerns, comments on interesting cases from his often crowded docket, as well as financial and personal issues crowd the pages of his letters. His most personal letters are directed to his wife, Alice, who he typically addressed as "My Dear Wife." These letters reveal what seems to have been a close and affectionate relationship. During one trip through the northern circuit of District Court for Taos and Rio Arriba County during May 1886, Judge Long closed his letters to Alice with numerous intimate phrases, such as "with a heart full of love and many kisses." One particularly lonely night from Taos, he concluded a lengthy description of the day's events with these words of endearment:

> I think of you very often, and am getting very anxious and more to receive a good warm loving kiss from your dear lips and an embrace from your loving breast. In your case the saying is reversed. It is 'out of sight but always in mind.' At every hour in the day my heart turns toward my dear wife with pleasing memories and deep love.

Judge Long also directed a number of letters to his children. On May 1, 1886, a few days before court convened at Taos, he stopped at Ojo Caliente to enjoy the hot mineral baths. From there, he wrote to his boys, Alfred and Bo, about a "cute little Mexican boy" he had observed. The boy was about twelve years old and had been caring for his family's flock of goats since he was six. The flock consisted of about fifty adult goats and a large number of kids. Every day, the nameless boy took his flock to the mountains for pasture. On one occasion, the boy and his faithful dog stopped to cross the river (Judge Long did not specify what river he referred to) a distance from the footbridge he usually used when the flock swam across. Judge Long and other observers wondered aloud how the boy would get to the other side. Their question was quickly answered as,

> The dog led the way into the river and the boy began to drive in the goats and they to swim across...when all at once, about two thirds of the flock being in and swimming, he seized one of the biggest goats, got on it leg upside and away he went into the river, the goat swimming and he riding to the other side. They went over safely and swimmingly. Don't you think he is a brave little boy?

In another letter to his sons, Judge Long described a visit to San Juan Pueblo (present-day Ohkay Owingeh) when he spent the night at the home of Samuel Eldolt, a prominent merchant from nearly Chamita. He described the inhabitants of San Juan as "...Indians, peaceable ones," who lived in three story mud houses, "built on top of one another – one house on top sets back from the edge of the under one about ten feet, then the next on top of that and back." Long was introduced to the Pueblo governor and his council, who agreed to "give a dance" in honor of their distinguished visitor. That evening, Long and his host went to the "council room" and the Indians began to dance:

> They had six musicians beating Tom, Toms, while the dancers with eagle feathers and paint on gave us the war dances. One old Indian with a big scalping knife bounced in the ring yelling, hi, hi, hi, brandishing his knife, and striking it on the floor in great style. This was the Ute war dance. It was quite a time. Colonel Johnson [an unidentified companion on the trip to Taos] took one of the Indian head feathers and put it on and gave them a white dance and the Indians laughed and said much fun.

These are but a few examples from Judge Long's wonderful collection of letters. These "voices from the past" provide us an intimate and rarely seen side of one of the important persons of territorial New Mexico. They help us see this particular frontier judge as an individual whose family was at least as important as his work inside the courtroom.

The Ordeal of a Free Black in Territorial New Mexico

Some time ago, I encountered an unusual and fascinating judicial case among records of the March 1861 term of Santa Fe County District Court. My attention was drawn to the case of "Territory of New Mexico – vs. - John Winters," in which the defendant was charged, convicted and imprisoned for being a "free Negro" living unlawfully in New Mexico.

The case surprised me, as I had long thought that after New Mexico became part of the United States, the territory was a "free state" in which emancipated black slaves could, and did, live freely. Spain had outlawed slavery in 1818, and Mexico itself reiterated the abolition "without exception" in 1837. Consequently, slavery was outlawed in New Mexico at the time we became part of the United States. A statement in our first proposed "state constitution" of 1848 reflected this anti-slavery tradition. "[We] do not desire to have domestic slavery within our borders," the document states, and petitions the U. S. Congress to assure that the territory would be protected against introduction of the institution.

The issue of slavery, however, came to the forefront in the ensuing debate and "Compromise of 1850" that admitted New Mexico as a territory. Subsequent political developments forced New Mexican officials to compromise their hard line against slavery. Given the choice to determine New Mexico's stand on the issue, subsequent territorial legislatures did not address Black slavery directly. Since a number of early American territorial officials, including some of the governors, owned slaves, the legislature chose instead to regulate only certain aspects of the issue, often pandering to Southern interests for political purposes. John Winters seems to have been an unwitting victim of such legislation.

Since the early 1850s and during the subsequent decade when President Abraham Lincoln issued the Emancipation Proclamation in 1863, only a few Black slaves actually lived in New Mexico. Most of these were owned by recently arrived Americans, some of whom were appointed to high offices in the territorial government. It is difficult to image why the few free Blacks in New Mexico such as John Winters would concern lawmakers. Winters had been in the territory since at least 1850, when the U. S. census shows he was living in Santa Fe. At that time, he was listed as age 28, a laborer, born in Virginia. Nine months later, on September 8, 1851, records of the Catholic Archdiocese of Santa Fe show Winters was baptized at the parish church in Santa Fe. Two weeks later, "Juan Tomas Wentes" married Josefa Moya in the same church.

Winters apparently made a life for himself in Santa Fe during the subsequent decade. The 1860 census shows him and Josefa still living in the city with their three children, owners of a modest personal estate. Josefa's parents, Juan and Encarnación Moya, lived a mere three houses away.

Whatever his life may have been up to that date, it was only a matter of time before the stark realities of the racism and territorial politics of the time caught up with him. On January 29, 1857, the territorial legislature passed "An Act Concerning Free Negroes" that made it illegal for a free Black man or mulatto to live in New Mexico. Violation of the statute and subsequent conviction could lead to a sentence of up to two years of hard labor in the penitentiary and a fine of at least fifty dollars. The legislation also prohibited the marriage of "any women of the white race of this territory" to the "aforesaid persons of color."

This legislation was clearly designed with men (as well as his children) such as John Winters in mind. It is impossible to tell why the law waited nearly four years to prosecute him. But it eventually did, and on March, 15, 1861, Winters was found guilty of the charges brought against him under provisions of the law. He was sentenced to one year of hard labor in the Santa Fe County jail and assessed the costs of prosecution.

I have not determined what became of John Winters and his family.

There was no territorial penitentiary in New Mexico at that time and no jail records exist that tell us how much time he actually served and whether he subsequently left New Mexico. The New Mexico legislature repealed the law "Concerning Free Negroes" in 1866, and I have not found anyone else prosecuted under this statute during the intervening years.

John Winters was convicted almost exactly a month before Fort Sumter was fired upon and the United States entered that dark period of our history known as the Civil War. It is tragic that on the eve of this monumental event, men such as John Winters were still feeling the burden of the racism that characterized that sad epoch of our history.

Juan Bautista Vigil y Alarid

On August 18, 1846, nearly one hundred and sixty years ago this month, General Stephen Watts Kearny and his Army of the West occupied Santa Fe without firing a shot. Governor Manuel Armijo had the day before fled south to Chihuahua. In the midst of what must have been an extraordinarily chaotic and distressing day for the residents of the city, Juan Bautista Vigil y Alarid was among the New Mexicans who stepped forward to face Kearny and deal with an uncertain future.

The following is my English translation of the speech Vigil y Alarid delivered to General Kearny on August 19, 1846. The original Spanish manuscript is found with the William G. Ritch Papers at the Huntington Library in San Marino California.

> My Lord General: The discourses your Excellency has delivered in taking possession of this county in the name of the United States of North America provide us an idea of the glorious future that awaits us. The question of deciding the boundaries of Nations does not fall to us - the cabinets of Mexico and Washington will decide their differences. To us falls the duty to obey and respect the established authorities despite our personal opinions. The sincere, honorable, and hardworking inhabitants of this Department offer their deference to the Government of North America. No one in this world has successfully resisted the power of the stronger. Your Excellency,

> do not think it strange that we have not manifested joy and enthusiasm in seeing our city occupied by your military forces. To us the political entity of the Mexican Republic has died. She, regardless of her circumstances, was our Mother. What son does not shed copious tears at the tomb of his parents? I could note some of the causes from whence came her dishonor, but domestic shortcomings should not be made public.
>
> Suffice it to say that a civil war is the unfortunate cause of the deadly poison that has spread over one of the best countries that has come from the hands of the Creator. Today we belong to a great and powerful Nation. The stars and stripes [that fly over] your command tent spread across the horizon of New Mexico: Its resplendent light spreads across this country like seed sown and cultivated on fertile land. We recognize by the moderation [demonstrated] by your Lordship, by the manners of your accommodating officers, and by the rigorous discipline of your troops, that we belong to the Republic that owes its origins to the immortal Washington, who is admired and respected by all civilized Nations. How different our fate would have been, had we been invaded by the European Nations. We know what the unfortunate Poles are enduring!
>
> In the name, then, of all the Department, I present obedience to the Republic of the North and offer to obey and respect its laws and authorities. Santa Fe, August 19, 1846
>
> Juan Bautista Vigil y Alarid, Governor.

How did it fall to him to deliver this speech and why did Vigil y Alarid attach the title of "Governor" to his elegant signature and rubric? It is well documented that Vigil y Alarid was the Secretary of Government under Governor Manuel Armijo at that fateful moment in our history. This was a significant position in the Mexican government, but it was not, as has been often suggested, the equivalent of being Lieutenant Governor or second in command. In the governor's absence, civil authority under the Mexican system was assumed by the *primer vocal* of the territorial *diputación*. So how did Vigil y Alarid end up with the title?

One explanation is that since Vigil y Alarid may have been the senior Mexican government official present in Santa Fe when the city was occupied, Kearny himself appointed him to the position. In his memoirs, Phillip St. George Cooke noted that Kearny appointed "temporary civil officers" on August 19, the same day Vigil y Alarid delivered his famous speech. The scant documentation of those hectic days, however, does not specify who these "temporary civil officers" were.

Vigil y Alarid's term as governor, whether actual or self-appointed, was short lived. On September 22, little more than a month after Kearny entered the city, Charles Bent was appointed governor. Following the Treaty of Guadalupe Hidalgo, Vigil y Alarid was among the several hundred New Mexicans who repatriated to Mexico. Research by Samuel Sisneros shows Vigil y Alarid was active in the northern Chihuahua community of Guadalupe through the 1850s. By 1860 he returned to New Mexico and provided important expert testimony in support of community land grant claims before the U. S. Surveyor General.

At a time of great crisis, Juan Bautista Vigil y Alarid stepped to the forefront and became immortalized with some of the most poignant and heartfelt words ever uttered in New Mexico history. One day someone will examine the full and extraordinary life of this civic leader and Mexican patriot.

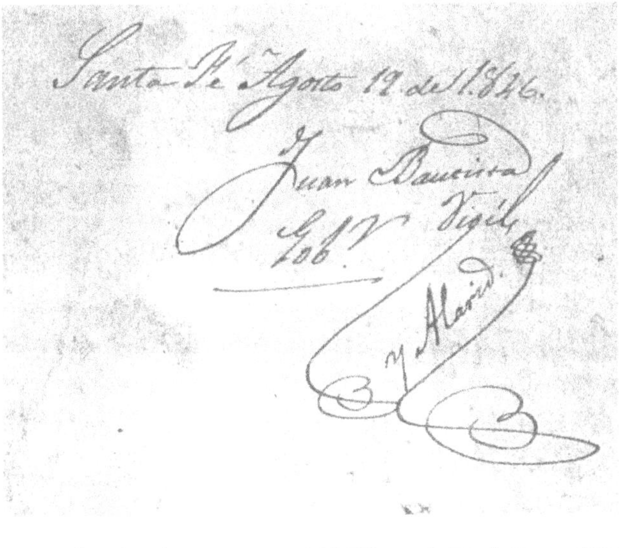

Juan Baptista Vigil y Alarid signature, 1846. William G. Ritch Papers (RI 241), Huntington Library, San Marino California

A Visit to Albuquerque in 1876

Sometime the late summer of 1876, an unnamed individual of the editorial staff of Santa Fe's *The Daily New Mexican* undertook a trip from Santa Fe to Albuquerque. An article featuring this trip was published in the September 28 issue of the paper. The two column article is a wonderful example of the promotional material that appeared in newspapers at a time when editors utilized their papers to promote development and immigration as much as they did the news.

The first part of the article is devoted to describing the telegraph line between Santa Fe and Albuquerque (which had lost its extra "r" by now). The telegraph had arrived in New Mexico in 1868 and the reporter's comments refer to recent improvements to the system. He described the line between the two cities as "a fine piece of work, symmetrical and durable," with poles of uniform size installed twenty five to the mile. The wire was of the heaviest type used and "securely fastened to glass insulators on strong brackets."

Most of the newspaper article, however, was devoted to describing the resources and some of the prominent residents of the region between the capital and Albuquerque. The reporter's first stops after leaving Santa Fe were at Pino's Ranch and Algodones, which he described as "good stopping places for both man and beast." The cultivated fields between these two sites were brimming with corn. He noted this had been a good year for farmers and that the wheat and oat crop had already been harvested.

On arriving at Bernalillo, he indicated this was where the "grape lands" of New Mexico commenced. From this point south, "innumerable vineyards enliven either side of the road and rejoice in their wealth of purple and white grape clusters…" The grape crop was "very luxuriant," contributing to an abundant harvest from which the "good wine" of the region was produced every year.

Bernalillo, Alameda and Albuquerque were also blessed with great orchards of apple, pear, peach, and plum trees that had produced more fruit this year than at any time in recent history. The heavily laden tree branches were bowed with "delicious sweets and [perfumed] the air with rare fragrance." In Albuquerque, the streets were lined with vendors selling fruit and an abundance of melons "at reasonable prices." The reporter also took the opportunity to visit the orchard of a "Mr. Bransford," who had cultivated a variety of fruit trees for ten years. The Bransford orchard was not very large, but he had carefully developed only the "choice varieties" of fruit trees. Mr. Bransford and his daughter were in the process of preparing large quantities of dried fruit for storage and later sale.

Albuquerque was described as "pleasantly situated on the east bank of the Rio Grande," but located some distance from the river itself. It should be noted that at the time of his visit, Albuquerque was limited to what we today call "old town," with the magnificent church of San Felipe de Neri standing on the north side of the traditional plaza. The railroad had not yet arrived in New Mexico, and today's "new town" had not yet developed east of the original Spanish settlement of *Alburquerque* (with the original spelling).

"Old town" Alburquerque, ca. 1900. Wood's Post Cards, Robert J. Tórrez Collection.

The reporter did not describe the plaza itself, but indicated the community had numerous well stocked stores, two good hotels and the *Review*, a weekly newspaper published by William M'Guinness. In the tongue-in-cheek style of the day, M'Guinness was described as "a wicked politician of the modern school of Democrats" (the *New Mexican* was published by staunch Republicans), whose saving grace was that he took "considerable pride" in Albuquerque and used his newspaper to promote the best interests of the city.

The unidentified reporter stayed at the Centennial Hotel, which he described as "a commodious hotel building." Mr. Warner, the owner, was commended for "setting a good table" and being the "model of a landlord." The other hotel in town, operated by Mr. Post, was also mentioned, but since he did not stay there, the reporter could only comment that it too, was "well spoken of."

The reporter says little else of Albuquerque. He does, however, make an observation that resonates loudly with recent concerns about the cottonwoods that are dying out along the middle Rio Grande valley. He described the large groves of cottonwood trees, "in their primal beauty," that formed a beautiful border along the banks of the river, in front of the farms and along the roads. He indicated that many young groves of cottonwoods were evident because this "swift-growing" tree was being planted along the river as a "protection to the river banks." It is interesting to note that the *bosque*, the wooded wetlands along the river, were as important to nineteenth century agriculture and ecology as it is to the future of the region.

The *U. S. S. New Mexico*

News releases and subsequent launching of the *U. S. S. New Mexico*, the United States Navy's newest Virginia–class submarine brought to mind the first major U. S. Navy ship named after our state. The battleship *U. S. S. New Mexico* was built in 1915 at the New York Navy Yard. At 32,000 tons and bristling with twelve fourteen inch guns, she and her sister ships, the *Mississippi* and *Idaho*, were among most powerful warships in the United States Navy.

The *U.S.S. New Mexico* was launched on April 13, 1917, with Miss Margaret C de Baca, daughter of the recently deceased New Mexico Governor Ezequiel C de Baca, in attendance as official sponsor. Moments after Miss C de Baca smashed the traditional bottle of champagne against the bow of the massive vessel, Virginia M. Carr, as maid of honor to the ceremony, broke a pottery jar filled with water from the Rio Grande and Pecos Rivers against the hull. In addition to Miss C de Baca several hundred additional New Mexicans were in attendance, including U. S. Senator A. A. Jones. Newspaper reports also identified Helen Kelly of Las Vegas, Irene Molinari of Portales, and Katherine French and Hildegarde Hurley of Santa Fe among the sponsors in attendance at the launching.

Launching of the U.S. S. New Mexico, 1917. New York Times, 27 April 1917.

Misses Margaret C de Baca, Virginia Carr and New Mexican delegation at launching of the U. S. S. New Mexico. New York Times, 27 April 1917.

After commissioning and initial training in 1918, the *New Mexico* departed for Brest, France, to escort the transport ship *George Washington* that carried President Woodrow Wilson from the Versailles Peace Conference.

That same summer, she was assigned as the flagship for the newly-organized Pacific Fleet and sailed immediately for the Panama Canal and port at San Pedro, California. For the next twelve years, *New Mexico* was occupied in frequent training maneuvers with the Atlantic fleet both in the Pacific and Caribbean. During this period, its ports-of –call included visits to several South American cities and a 1925 cruise to Australia and New Zealand.

New Mexico was overhauled and modernized between 1931 and 1933 after which she returned to the Pacific in 1934. She was based at Pearl Harbor as World War II broke out in Europe. In the summer of 1941 she sailed to join the Atlantic fleet for duty on neutrality patrol, but when the Japanese attacked Pearl Harbor on December 7, she was ordered back to the Pacific. For the first part of the war, *New Mexico* conducted troop transport escort and participated in the campaign against the Japanese in the Aleutian Islands. She then participated in the bombardment and assault on the Gilbert and Marshall Islands. In June 1944 she bombarded Tinan, Saipan, and Guam on consecutive days, and on June 18, twice helped fight off enemy air attacks.

In October 1944, *New Mexico* underwent an overhaul and by November, returned to action at the Leyte Gulf where she protected reinforcement and supply convoys, fighting off the desperate daily air assaults that characterized Japanese resistance to the impending American invasion of the Philippines. Her next major operation was the invasion of Luzon, where on January 6, 1945, one of the Japanese suicide planes found its way through her anti-aircraft defenses and crashed into her bridge. The ship's commanding officer, Captain R. W. Fleming and twenty- nine of her crew were killed. Her guns, however, remained in action while the damage was repaired.

After undergoing repairs at Pearl Harbor, *New Mexico* returned to action in support of the invasion of Okinawa. From March 26 through April 17, her guns remained in constant support of the troops engaged onshore. On May 12, however, she was attacked by two suicide aircraft just after sunset. One of the attackers crashed into her while the other managed to hit her with its bomb. The ensuing explosions and fire killed fifty -four of her crew and wounded 119 others. She was removed to Leyte for repairs and was being outfitted and her crew undergoing training for the impending invasion of the Japanese home islands when Japan surrendered on August 14, 1845. New Mexico and her crew were present at Tokyo Bay to witness the formal Japanese surrender on September 2.

New Mexico's namesake battleship received six battle stars for its service in World War II. Its glorious record, however, did not save it from the ignominious fate of old battlewagons. A poem entitled *A Ghost Ship!* noted *New Mexico's* impending fate:

Her empty hull now silent
The ships bell will ring no more
She is slated for scrap iron
When she would reach the shore

The ship's too old and slow they say,
She was the best in her day
Her tearful crew had said goodbye
The time had come for her to die

After docking at Boston Harbor on October 17, 1945, the *U. S. S. New Mexico* was decommissioned the following summer and sold for scrap a year later.

The Railroad arrives in New Mexico

The railroad was coming! As the Atchison, Topeka & Santa Fe Railway made its way across the northern New Mexico mountains over Raton Pass in late December 1878, every New Mexico town eagerly anticipated the day the railroad would arrive in their community. When the AT&SF chugged into Las Vegas on July 4, 1879, the *Las Vegas Gazette* reported that a stand for speakers had been erected in the plaza, homes and business were decorated with flags, and the entire town enjoyed "a general holiday appearance." The paper continued:

> At the depot, the surroundings were a patriotic aspect. Two locomotives came in dressed out in flags and furbelowed in the highest style of art. Large United States and Mexican flags adorned their grim visaged fronts while smaller flags and streamers completed the attire. During the day thousands of people visited them and curiously inspected their powerful mechanism.

When the railroad reached the territorial capital at Santa Fe less than a year later, an enthusiastic and festive procession formed on the historic plaza and made its way across the river to await the arrival of the first locomotive into the city. At the appointed hour of noon, the announcement was made that the last spike was to be driven and several prominent officials accompanied Governor Lew Wallace to take a few swings at the spike and complete the much anticipated railroad that linked New Mexico's capital to the modern world. *The New Mexican* hailed "SANTA FE'S TRIUMPH!" and declared that at long last, "The Last Link is Forged in the Iron Chain which Binds the Ancient City to the United States."

SANTA FE'S TRIUMPH!

The Last Link is Forged in the Iron Chain which Binds the Ancient City to the United States.

And The Old Santa Fe Trail Passes into Oblivion.

An Immense Crowd Greets the Coming of the Iron Steed.

Speeches and Congratulations!!

Headlines, Santa Fe New Mexican, February 9, 1880.

Soon it was Albuquerque's turn, and the community could hardly contain its excitement. "Almost here" declared the April 3, 1880 issue of *The Albuquerque Review* in bold letters. The construction locomotive "was puffing and fizzing about half a mile south of don Juan Cristobal Armijo's house," placing the advancing railroad track south of Bernalillo and about two miles north of the city. The paper optimistically predicted that when the train arrived, it would be "the day from which Albuquerque may reasonably expect to date the commencement of her material prosperity and the beginning of her existence as the Queen City of the Rio Grande."

Prominent citizens quickly convened a public meeting to discuss arrangements for a proper commemoration of the event. Committees were appointed to contact representatives of the railroad company to determine when the first train was actually expected to arrive in Albuquerque so that city officials could arrange a grand welcome and offer the "congratulations of the people of Albuquerque." Invitations had to be sent to prominent citizens of the territory, speakers had to be found, arrangements made for music, and above all, funds were needed to pay for the celebration. According to a list of "Subscribers to the Railroad Celebration" published in the April 24, 1880 issue of the *Review* a total of $420.20 was contributed by several dozen donors. Major donors included Franz Huning, Stover & Co., Santiago Baca and Ambrosio Armijo.

Although the rail line had arrived several days earlier, at high noon on April 22, 1880, the roar of a canon signaled the "formal opening of the A. T. & S. F. R.R. to public traffic" and the celebration was under way. The Ninth Cavalry (Colored) Regiment band provided lively music while officials and families in brightly decorated carriages formed a procession to the depot where the presiding officers mounted two flatbed cars that served as a stage for the occasion. The assembled crown cheered as a special train arrived, carrying more than four hundred invited guests from Santa Fe, Bernalillo, "and other points." Eloquent speeches were delivered by Judge William Hazledine, Colonel José F. Chávez, Rev. Donato Gasparri, S.J., and Tranquilino Luna. Later, a stream of carriages carried guests to the plaza while an "excursion train" consisting of four passenger cars and five flatbed cars crowded to capacity with enthusiastic "pleasure seekers" made a special trip to Bernalillo and back. The *Review* noted that two-thirds of these passengers had never before ridden on a train.

That evening bonfires illuminated the plaza while the Ninth Cavalry band provided entertainment to the vast crowd gathered for the occasion. More speeches were punctuated by the loud boom of a small canon while "skyrockets and bombs shot through the air." Finally, at nine o'clock that evening the visitors returned to the depot for the return trip to Santa Fe and other points north. The crowd at the plaza no doubt lingered to listen to music, visit with friends and neighbors and muse over Albuquerque's promising future. As the *Weekly New Mexican* noted in their report of "Albuquerque's Gala Day," arrival of the railroad had assured the city's future and quipped that "Adelante [Forward], Albuquerque," would henceforth be its motto.

A Ride on the D&RG, 1911

In late November 1911, an unidentified reporter for the *Santa Fe New Mexican* took a trip on the Denver and Rio Grande narrow gauge railroad from the capital in Santa Fe to the northern New Mexico community of Chama. He wrote about his journey in a series of articles published in late November and early December of that year. His account of the two-day trip through the mountains of northern New Mexico is filled with a sense of adventure as well as names of places and distinguished travelers he encountered along the way.

D&RG Train near Antonito, Colorado, 1880s. B. W. Kilburn 5453, "Trip to New Mexico" Stereograph. Robert J. Tórrez Collection.

The train left Santa Fe shortly after ten o'clock in the morning of the first day of the trip and arrived at Antonito, Colorado, at an unspecified time that evening after dark. Along the way, the reporter noted many distinguished passengers that boarded and departed the train at Española, Santa Cruz and Barranca. The passengers included New Mexico's delegate to the U. S. Congress, William H. Andrews and three well-known members of the clergy, including the Rev. Joséph Pugens and Rev. Joséph Pajot. At Santa Cruz, territorial legislator Julian Trujillo boarded the train to greet Mr. Andrews. Along the route north of Española at La Joya (today's Velarde), the train passed the "Sunshine Ranch" of former governor L. Bradford Prince, whose orchards were considered among the finest in the territory. At dinnertime, a stop at Embudo was particularly appreciated. Several passengers apparently lingered over the apple pie they were served for dessert and nearly missed the departing train.

At Antonito, Colorado, most of the passengers spent the night at the Palace Hotel. The hotel's steam heat and electric lights broke the chill of the high country air and darkness of this remote community. A pianist in the dining parlor of the hotel and a mechanical phonograph in the upper floor helped make their brief stay in southern Colorado town a pleasant one.

The following morning, the D&RG began what everyone anticipated would be a harrowing trip over the mountains to Chama. The potential dangers prompted one passenger to offer a prayer that all would reach Chama safely, then began to tell stories of train wreaks that sent engines and passenger cars careening down the mountainsides "with the dash and recklessness of toboggans." Others told of trains stranded for days in the mountains by heavy snowfalls or avalanches that blocked the tracks. The presence of snow sheds and snow fences along the route only served to heighten anxiety among some of the passengers. One seasoned traveler indicated he had been on a train that spent two nights in a snow shed near the summit. To pass the time and console the children through this harrowing experience, the passengers had organized a minstrel show that everyone apparently enjoyed and appreciated. These stories prompted some passengers to make a mental inventory of the supplies they had available in case the train became stranded.

TRAVELING NORTH
BY THE D. R. G.

Vastness of Empire of New Mexico Is Thus Fully Realized

GOOD APPLE PIE AT EMBUDO

And Wonderful Violet Tints of Taos Skies Make Trip Agreeable.

Headlines from the SFNM

The circuitous route of the narrow gauge tracks along mountain ledges, through tunnels and the many "tortuous turns" were a constant source of amazement and discussion. One passenger told of his trip over this route the previous year during Thanksgiving and of having observed a barn dance at a well-lit house. The music and gaiety could be heard and seen from the train as it passed nearby. As they left this scene behind, they soon observed another dance and finally, a third. "My," remarked one amazed passenger, "I wonder if all the people on this mountain are dancing tonight?" She could hardly believe that it was actually the same dance, observed from different vantage points as the track wound its way through the many hairpin turns that characterize the D&RG rail line through the mountains.

The train reached Chama that evening without incident or delay. The passengers debarked and filed into a nearly hotel where they eagerly dispatched a welcome, if not tasty, dinner of "boiled chicken and minced pie."

At this point, the reporter departed from the train and joined a party of local dignitaries led by Thomas D. Burns, one of Rio Arriba County's most prominent merchants and influential political figures. Burns, District Attorney Alexander Read and Rio Arriba County Treasurer (and later Representative to the U. S. Congress), Benigno C. Hernández met delegate Andrews and escorted him to Burns' home in Tierra Amarilla. The balance of the article is devoted to extolling the resources of the Tierra Amarilla area and the extent of Burns' holdings and influence. The unnamed reporter's often tongue-in-cheek account of his trip provides us with an extraordinary account of one way New Mexicans traveled at a time when the territory was on the verge of finally becoming a full fledged member of the American Union.

El Año de la Nevada

Heavy snowfalls and news of the hardships that deep accumulation of snow imposed on individuals and communities in northern New Mexico recall one of the most severe winters of the twentieth century – the winter of 1931-1932. That winter has become known in New Mexico folklore as *el año de la nevada,* the year of the great snowfall.

The *Santa Fe New Mexican* of November 23, 1931, provides an early hint of the trouble brewing in northern New Mexico when it reported "Roads into Rio Arriba Blocked." The paper reported four feet of snow had accumulated in Chama by 4:00 P. M. the previous day - and it was still falling. All roads into the area were blocked by the snow despite the highway department's best efforts to break though.

The memory of that year's snowfall is strong in the oral histories and recollections of those who lived through it. Kenneth R. Lively, a long-time resident and merchant in Chama recalled that more than forty- one feet of snow were measured at Cumbres Pass that winter of 1931-32 and that ten feet of that snow had accumulated in the ten day period between November 10th and 20th, 1931. Climatological records from the Chama station show unusually high levels of total precipitation for the period September through December of 1931, with 4.13 inches recorded in November of that year. The greatest tragedy of that year's snowfall, according to oral history, is that the vast accumulation of late 1931 was followed by very cold temperatures that kept the snow from melting. Then another major storm hit in February of 1932, compounding the problem. Precipitation records from Chama confirm 4.60 inches of precipitation for February 1932 – more than was recorded for November of the previous year!

Based on recollections of those who lived through the experience, the tragedy of that year came from what the storms did to livestock and consequently, to the livelihood of many people throughout New Mexico. By all accounts, people in northern Rio Arriba are used to dealing with heavy snows – that is, when Mother Nature played fair. Under normal conditions, snow fell, the weather improved, the snow melted, and man and beast got through it just fine until the next storm. In 1931 the November snowfall accumulated quickly and melted slowly. That winter, my father, José D. Tórrez, was living at Diamante, a cluster of ranches and homesteads located northwest of Chama. He recalled that it began snowing heavily about 4:00 one afternoon and by the following morning the snow was so deep, they could not open the doors to the house. Local tradition indicates that one vast snowfall occurred the night of November 17, 1931. Dad recalled literally having to dig tunnels through the drifts to get firewood and do what they could for the livestock. Horses had to be used to break through the snow to allow sheep and cattle to get to feed. He recalled many sheep men were moving their flocks to winter grazing at "el Navajo" in western New Mexico when the great storm hit. Many came home literally empty-handed – they had lost everything.

The great tragedy of the "año de la nevada" comes from this great loss of sheep and other livestock. The losses were compounded by the fact that many of these sheep men had their sheep on *partido* – a system of shares in which they would literally lease a flock of sheep from a livestock owner on the promise of paying them back with a certain number of "new" ewes every year as well as a percentage of the wool clip and lambs every spring. This system worked reasonably well when conditions and pasture were good, but during the winter of 1931- 32, things went terribly wrong.

The Rev. Aloysius Albrecht, OFM, pastor at San José Parish in Los Ojos described the problem in a letter he wrote to *St. Anthony's Messenger* the following year:

> Last winter [1931] all the people who had sheep suffered tremendous losses. The herders were caught with their flocks in the early snow as they were on their way to lower and warmer grazing…the loss was between [35 and 50 percent] and in some areas it was so great that the sheep men lost everything

> they had. Many were obliged to borrow money from the bank to buy food, and the only way they could pay their debts was to turn over their mortgaged sheep to the bank. Now they are without sheep and without employment.

My father recalled fragments of some verses from *corridos*, ballads that were written soon after the tragic events of that winter. Their simplicity reflects best the sentiment of northern New Mexico's citizens about that terrible winter of 1931 -1932 – the infamous and unforgettable *año de la Nevada*.

El '29 compró baraja	'29 bought the playing cards
El '30 las varajió	'30 shuffled them
El '31 echó monte, y	'31 dealt monte, and
El '32 nos tapó	'32 covered us
Le quedaron sus piales	He retained his ropes and lariats
Y sus sillas,	as well as his saddles,
Pero vacillos sus corrales	But his corrales were empty

Fabian García, Pioneer Horticulturalist.

Imagine what your last visit to a favorite Mexican food restaurant would be without the obligatory question from the waiter, "Red or Green?" As much as we take such variety for granted, it might be said that New Mexico's "Official Question" would not be possible without the pioneering work of one of New Mexico's underappreciated heroes – Fabian García. Fabian García was a pioneering horticulturalist and the first director of what is now Mexico State University's Agricultural Experiment Station in Las Cruces. In 1907, García began his experiments in chile-breeding that led to the 1921 release of "New Mexico No. 9," the first standard variety of the chile pepper we are so familiar with today.

According to information found in the NMSU web site, the "No. 9" was the first chile pod that farmers could depend on to grow into a consistent and predictable (and therefore more marketable) pepper in terms of size and "heat." Before then, cultivated chiles were much smaller and came in a "bewildering" variety of sizes and shapes that made it impossible for farmers to determine what size or variety of chile they were planting from year to year. Chile grown in New Mexico – the long green pod that turns red in the fall – was well adapted to New Mexico. This was especially true in the Chimayo and Española valleys of northern New Mexico, where ancient varieties are still grown today, but were often deemed unsuitable for mass production. García experimented with three chile types – the *chile negro*, a dark, almost black variety; the *chile colorado* of the Chimayo type; and the *chile parella*, dark brown in color, long and thin, almost like a pencil. From these he developed the size and shape of the chile pod we are familiar with today.

Fabian García was born in Chihuahua, Mexico in 1871. Orphaned while still an infant, he was brought to the United States by his grandmother in 1873 and settled in the community of San Lorenzo, west of Silver City, where she worked as a domestic. He and his grandmother later moved to Georgetown, the mining town where a young Fabian developed into the "champion marble player of the vicinity."

Fabian Garcia. Photo by Ruliene E. Banner, Courtesy of Rio Grande Historical Collections, New Mexico State University, #0071004.

Fabian's future took a fortuitous turn when his grandmother took a position with the prominent Thomas Casad family south of Mesilla. The Casad family provided Fabian with a private tutor and sent him to what was then Las Cruces College. Although he was not considered "a talented student," he graduated in 1894, having served as president of the Columbian Literary Society and a member of the college's first football team. He followed his undergraduate work with a year at Cornell University before returning to the New Mexico College of Agriculture and Mechanical Arts for the remainder of his long and distinguished career.

After obtaining his M.S.A. degree at NMSU in 1906, he held the position of "Professor of Horticulture" until 1945, serving as Director of the Agricultural Experiment Station for more than three decades. Besides his pioneering work on chile, he is credited with introducing the "Grano onion" and planting some of the first pecan trees in the Mesilla Valley in 1913. Nearly three dozen varieties of the pecan trees he planted are said to still stand today, pioneers of the extensive pecan orchards that have become such as large part of the agricultural industry in the Mesilla Valley.

Little is written about Dr. García's personal life (he was awarded an honorary doctorate from the University of New Mexico in 1943). In 1907 he married Julieta Amador, daughter of one of the Mesilla Valley's most prominent families. The couple apparently had one son, who died while an infant. Doña Julieta died in 1920 and García never remarried.

He is remembered as a talented administrator with a remarkable sense of humor. He never lost touch with his humble beginnings and maintained a fierce pride in his Mexican heritage. "Don't be afraid to say you're Mexican," he would tell his students. "I came from Mexico and I'm proud of it." Don Fabian died in 1948 following a long and debilitating struggle with Parkinson's disease. His will directed that the bulk of his estate, worth an estimated $85,000, be left to NMSU to build a dormitory on the campus for use by deserving, Spanish-surnamed students. In addition to "García Hall," the NMSU dormitory built in 1967 that bears his name, students and faculty conduct research in horticulture and agronomy at the "Fabian García Science Center" located on the university's farm. A fitting tribute, perhaps, to a New Mexican whose plaque at the American Society of Horticulture Hall of Fame bears the words, "Dr. Fabian García, a man of humble origins but a gentleman of extraordinary achievements." He may also be known to us at the "Father of the Mexican Food Industry."

A number of photographs and more information about Dr. García's life can be found in the New Mexico State University Rio Grande Historical Collections website at www.nmsu.edu.

The Las Vegas Fire of 1880

"Lurid Las Vegas" read the headlines of the September 19, 1880 issue of the *Daily New Mexican.* The story that followed was an early report taken from the *Daily Optic* that Las Vegas' "new town," what we know today as East Las Vegas, had just been "Laid in Ruins by Fire." Quoting the Las Vegas paper, the *New Mexican* relayed news that "The most disastrous fire that ever fell to the lot of our noble town, broke out in Walter E. Marble's residence ... at 4 o'clock this afternoon [September 18]."

Early reports indicated the fire had started in the frame building that housed Marble's grocery store and his personal residence. Citizens and neighbors gathered quickly to pour water on the fire, but the building went up in flames and quickly spread to an adjacent Chinese laundry and then to Marcus & Clem's grocery. The best anyone could do was move store merchandise onto the street to keep it from being consumed by the "onward march of the Fire King." Firefighters quickly realized that the whole block fronting Railroad Avenue would soon go up in flames and efforts shifted to save the warehouses of commercial giants Browne & Manzanares and Otero, Sellar & Co., which were located directly across the street from the burning buildings. Armed with "Babcock extinguishers," a bucket brigade kept the walls of the warehouses dowsed with water to protect them from flames. "It was with the most superhuman efforts that either of these large establishments were saved," reported the following day's *Optic,* "and their salvation is due to the brave boys who faced the danger and fought heroicly (sic) – fought until their feet, hands and faces were blistered by the extreme heat."

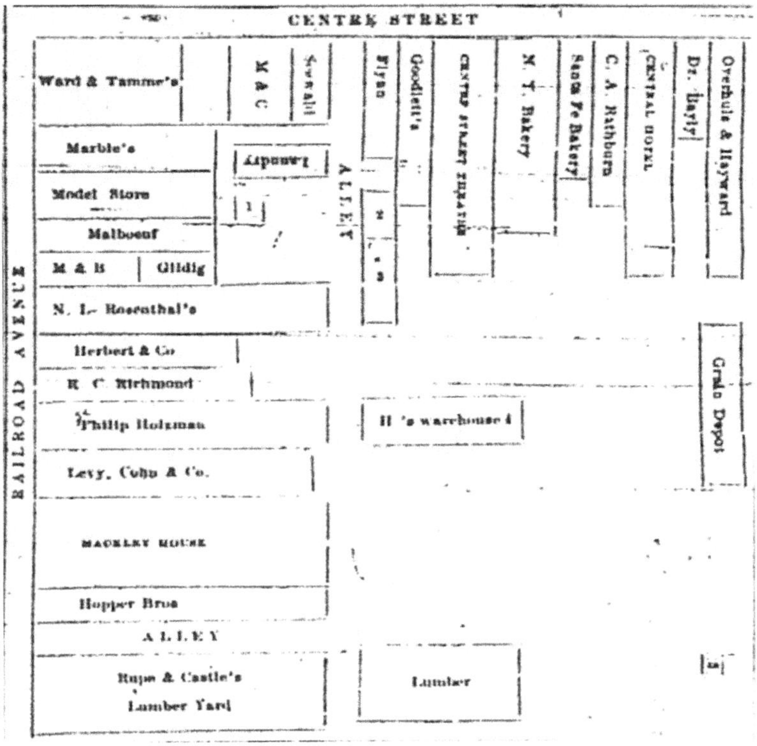

"The Burnt District," Las Vegas Daily Optic, 20 September 1880.

[below] Babcock fire extinguisher from 1872 company advertisement.

The fire consumed an entire city block within an hour. Part of the problem was caused by a limited supply of water - the papers do not tell us whether it came from a municipal source or private wells. Numerous devices were utilized to stem the advance of the flames. Barrels of dampened salt were hoisted onto the roofs and spread on the roof tiles; blankets, carpets and canvas were soaked with water and spread on the roofs; one building was even dynamited. The *Optic* reported that a keg of gunpowder was placed in Phillip Holzman's store and the fuse lit in order to blow out the building and try to stem the advancing flames along Railroad Avenue. However, a volunteer, unaware of the plan, spotted the "deadly agent," defused the keg, and threw it out into the street. By the time firefighters realized what had happened, the Holzman store was consumed by the advancing fire. Their initial plan thwarted, the firefighters moved the gunpowder keg two buildings down to the "Mackley House" and succeeded in setting off the charge. The explosion blew the roof off the store and collapsed part of the building. The ploy worked. The advancing flames were slowed and the adjacent building of Rupe & Castle was saved, except for some damage, which may have been caused by the blast, to its sales room.

Once the fire was contained attention turned to another immediate problem – control and capture of numerous "light-fingered" thieves who had taken advantage of the confusion and frantic activity to steal whatever they could from the goods being saved from the fire and placed onto the streets. "Plunder and rapine," noted the *Optic,* "were carried on to such an extent that not more than one-fourth of the saved property escaped the clutches of the unlawful." Twenty five uniformed "San Miguel Rifles," the local militia, patrolled throughout the night, saving thousands of dollars of goods and merchandise from the thieves. The militia succeeded in arresting a number of the suspected thieves, and by morning the "little East Side calaboose was comfortably filled…" The papers listed several names of those who apparently were brought before a justice of the peace and fined ten to fifteen dollars each.

The *Optic* praised several individuals whose efforts to fight the fire were "above and beyond." George Carlin, a waiter at the St. Nicholas Hotel, "with a commendable nerve, fought the demon open-handed." Charlie Stewart and Martin, (no last name given), both "colored" employees at the same hotel, were also singled out for their bravery. Several persons suffered burns, but no loss of life was reported. Interestingly, most of the injuries seem to have been caused by falling debris or objects thrown from burning buildings. All those burned and injured were expected to recover.

In all, nearly forty business and several homes were destroyed. Losses were estimated at more than $100,000 and dozens of residents were left homeless. Reports indicate a percentage of the losses were covered by insurance and that despite the destruction, by the following day some of the merchants were setting up shop in other locations and others were already clearing the debris and making plans to rebuild. As the *Daily Optic* predicted "The Phoenix is Rising from its Ashes Sure Enough!"

A Protest by Chimayo Weavers

Chimayo weaver at his loom. HMC Post card, Robert J. Tórrez Collection

In early January 1908, the governing board of the New Mexico Territorial Penitentiary was considering the introduction of carpet weaving as a type of work which could be done by convict labor. It was felt that weaving would be a valuable skill which could be learned by convicts and would complement the brick making and road labor projects already established at the penitentiary. The Board seemed convinced this type of industry would be especially adapted to the southwest because the territory already produced most of the raw materials used by the territory's many blanket and rug weavers.

There was even some optimism expressed that if the weaving project was successful, it could lead to the establishment of a carpet weaving industry in New Mexico. "New Mexico imports too much," noted the *Santa Fe New Mexican*, "and in consequence grows too little along industrial lines and no means that promise to change this untoward condition should be neglected or deemed too visionary for at least a trial." Any expectations for the project, however, were quickly dashed by events which followed soon after the penitentiary's plans were announced.

A few days after the story appeared in the paper, Victor Ortega, a prominent merchant and postmaster at Chimayo, wrote to attorney Thomas B. Catron in Santa Fe. Ortega advised Catron that a number of weavers had approached him and asked if he would check into the story they had heard of the plans to install a weaving industry at the penitentiary. They also presented a petition with more than fifty signatures which claimed that such an industry would be detrimental to their own livelihoods as weavers. These individuals, Ortega noted, were "weavers of blankets which they sell at low prices which barely allow them to make a living." Ortega asked Catron to forward the weaver's petition to the governor and do all he could to convince the governor and the Board of Penitentiary Commissioners to institute some other project which would not be so prejudicial to the interests of New Mexico's citizens.

It is difficult to tell what influence Catron's letter had on Governor George Curry, who served as Chairman of the Penitentiary Board. Catron did not specifically suggest Curry stop the plans, but indicated that maybe some other manufacture be considered which would "not come in conflict with private enterprises of people who are not of the convict class." In his response to Catron, Governor Curry reiterated the government's desire to establish prison industries that provided work for the convicts and also reduced "the expenses of the institution." However, he did not want this goal to interfere or compete with private enterprise, and consequently, assured Catron that, "nothing will be done to compete with the people of Rio Arriba, or any other county in the territory, in their manufacture of blankets." Curry's letter ended any prospects of establishing a weaving project at the penitentiary.

Several questions arise from this seemingly insignificant incident in New Mexico's long and colorful history. The relative ease with which the project was dropped makes one wonder how serious the penitentiary administration was about the project. Was Curry's decision to drop the project simply a move to cultivate some good will (and maybe a few votes) in Rio Arriba County, or was it that the project may have in fact impacted the weaving industry?

Certainly, if the signatures on the petition were all weavers, this would have reflected a significant portion of the population. The 1910 census, for example, makes it clear that weavers were an important part of the economy in the Chimayo area. A cursory review of the population listing for Rio Arriba's Chimayo census precinct number four, shows the residents of Chimayo held the vast range of occupations common to that time. The listing of occupations include teachers, store owners, coal miners, lumber workers, laborers, farmers, shepherds, ranchers and of course, weavers. This precinct alone shows at least nineteen households in which one or more persons earned their livelihood "making blankets." The households of Juan Baca and Blas Martinez, for example, show three persons in each of these families were weavers.

It appears that the weavers of Chimayo were correct in concluding that the plans for a weaving program at the penitentiary would probably have had a detrimental effect on their own livelihood. Their petition asking for due consideration is another example of how our New Mexican ancestors were not shy about exercising a little political influence to protect their interests. The survival of the weaving industry in Chimayo is a loud testament to their efforts.

Personal Tragedies

In my research into the extensive judicial records maintained at our state archives, I am often amazed at the number of cases one comes across that involve women. I have also found a number of these cases in which closer examination of the records and related newspaper reports show that certain women whose names show up in judicial records were not actually involved in criminal activity, but came to the attention of public authorities and entered the public record because of tragic personal circumstances and accidents.

One of these is the story of Sarah Lizzie Beckworth. The December 12, 1885 issue of *The Leader*, a Santa Fe newspaper, reported that Beckworth, who resided at Cerrillos, was being held in the Santa Fe County jail, charged with the murder of her young son. Sarah's case came to public attention when she pleaded with neighbors to help her dying infant. Neighbors found the child malnourished and with burn blisters on the soles of his feet and immediately suspected Sarah had inflicted the injuries. The newspaper report indicated neighbors who saw the dying infant speculated the child had starved, died as a result of the burns, or was poisoned by the distraught mother. Under the circumstances, Lizzie was arrested and charged with murder.

However, subsequent investigation revealed the boy had recently suffered a bout of scarlet fever from which he never fully recovered. The burns were the result of a desperate attempt by his mother to provide a bizarre treatment in which she applied a mustard plaster to the child's soles and then held his feet close to a fire so that the heat would somehow enable the treatment to take effect. The resulting burns festered, apparently became infected, and combined with the lingering effects of the scarlet fever and malnourishment due to the mother's impoverished condition, the child subsequently died. When the investigation was completed, one Santa Fe County official noted that the whole incident was, at worse, "a terrible misfortune, but not the poor woman's fault." When her case came before the Santa Fe County Grand Jury, they returned a "No true bill." In an unusual comment added to their refusal to indict her, the grand jury urged the District Attorney and judge to petition the County Commission to do what it could to help her. Sarah Lizzie Beckworth, was in their eyes, not a criminal, but "purely an object of charity, and that the County of this Territory should make provisions for her maintenance."

A similar criminal case in 1887 was brought before a Bernalillo County grand jury in 1887 charging Josefa Lobato with the murder of a two or three year old boy whose remains were found partially buried in a pig pen behind her house in Bernalillo. Suspicions fell on the woman when a young boy (whose relationship to her was not well established, but it apparently was not her son) she was raising was noticed missing. She told officials the boy was with relatives at the Pueblo of Sandia, but subsequent investigation failed to find the boy until a local sheepherder stumbled onto his partially buried remains in a pig pen located in a corral behind Josefa's home. Testimony taken at a hearing held by Justice of the Peace Manuel García gathered enough evidence to order her arrest and confine her to jail until the upcoming district court grand jury term. Her bond was set at $1,500.

Despite the unexplained nature of the boy's death and some lurid publicity surrounding the case, such as the *Albuquerque Morning Democrat* headlines of the story which read, "Horrible Particulars of the Atrocious Crime Committed at Bernalillo," a grand jury failed to indict Josefa for murder. The jury apparently believed her story that the boy had died suddenly and being a poor woman without the resources to bury the child properly and ashamed to ask for charity, decided to bury the body in her own back yard. The actual reason for the failure of the grand jury to indict Josefa Lobato is not reflected in the criminal case file. The official record simply states that they found "No true bill" and Josefa was presumably released. We can only assume that while the jury may have been appalled by the gruesome nature of the child's burial and subsequent discovery, they found no criminal intent in the boy's death and believed that Josefa's story was completely plausible.

Our Spanish, Mexican and Territorial archives contain many fascinating and often tragic examples of women that show up in the historical record because of unfortunate circumstances. As we read about these women from our past, we need to keep in mind that our ancestors often lived lives that were much more difficult than we could ever imagine. Sarah and Josefa were not 'bad girls' in the moral sense that the newspaper headlines of the time may have initially implied, but rather that they suffered more than most from the same human tragedies that have plagued us throughout history.

The Four Deaths of Governor George Curry

Governor George Curry. Portrial by Sam Smith, Old Lincoln County Memorial Commission (dev.newmexico.org).

George Curry was one of New Mexico's most colorful characters. Born in Louisiana in 1861, Curry was working as a clerk in Dodge City, Kansas, when he first came to New Mexico in 1875 with his uncle as part of a wagon train delivering freight to Fort Union. In 1879, he decided the "lure of Lincoln County" was too much to resist and moved permanently to New Mexico. Over the next decade he was an active participant in the rough and tumble "wild west" events of time, including a casual encounter with Billy the Kid himself.

Curry was first elected to political office in 1888, when he won the position of Lincoln County Clerk. He was later elected Sheriff and then in 1894, to the territorial senate representing the legislative district that included Lincoln, Chaves and Eddy Counties. When the Spanish-American War broke out in 1898, he enlisted in Theodore Roosevelt's "Rough Riders."Although he did not see any action in that war, he later served in the Philippines, holding offices of Chief of Police in Manila and provincial governor. In 1907 he was appointed Governor of New Mexico by President Theodore Roosevelt, an old "Rough Rider" friend. After serving as territorial governor from 1907 to 1910, he went on to lead a full and active life for several decades. In 1945, Governor John Dempsey appointed him New Mexico's first official State Historian, a position he held until his death at the Veteran's Hospital in Albuquerque on November 27, 1947. The newspaper reports of his death review his many accomplishments and published glowing obituaries that reflected his long and eventful life. The catch was that his death had been reported at least three times before.

George Curry's first death was reported in 1884, while he was still a robust young man. According to his own telling of the story, he was sharing a hotel room in Raton with an Englishman who had the bad habit of "flashing his bank roll." One morning the Englishman left the room after putting on Curry's vest by mistake. That afternoon, the Englishman was murdered, and when his body was found, the only identification they found on him was a letter addressed to George Curry. Lacking further information, a coroner's jury ruled that "George Curry came to his death at the hands of persons unknown" and a flowery obituary was published in a local newspaper. In his autobiography, Governor Curry quipped that the justice of the peace that had presided at the inquest in 1884 attended his inauguration as governor in 1907. When he went through the receiving line the man told Governor

Curry that he had come to see if it was true he was alive.

The second report of his premature death came in 1905 while he was in the Philippines. He had apparently gone missing after a battle with rebel forces and presumed killed. When he showed up safe and sound and returned to headquarters, he found a cablegram from President Theodore Roosevelt congratulating him on a "miraculous escape."

The third and next to last, report of Governor Curry's premature death came the morning of April 12, 1932. That day the *Albuquerque Journal*'s morning headlines reported that former Governor Curry had died at Hillsboro the day before. The paper indicated that attending physicians had reported his death "was brought about by natural causes, though it came unexpectedly." The paper even reported plans had been made for "unpretentious" services and burial at the community cemetery in Hillsboro.

That same day, however, headlines in Santa Fe's *New Mexican* (which was then an afternoon paper), read "Governor George Curry Says Report of Death Exaggerated." The former governor apparently took the news of his death in good humor and reportedly quipped, "There is virtually no basis whatsoever for the report of my death." In a good natured exchange with reporters, Curry was asked, "How dead are you Governor?" To which he responded, "I don't what to disappoint you boys and I know there must be at least 2 per cent truth in any newspaper story. But as a matter of fact I am not very dead – hardly dead enough to mention." He hoped the report of his death would be corrected, noting, "my friends might be worried about it."

Three times Governor Curry had the opportunity to know how Mark Twain felt when he quipped about his own obituary. In his autobiography, *George Curry 1861-1947, An Autobiography*, first published posthumously in 1957, Curry indicated he never did find out how the rumor of his third premature death got started. The next time his death is reported, he concluded "I expect the report will be correct…my years have mounted…and the years have taken their toll." Governor Curry had been in the Veteran's Hospital in Albuquerque for three weeks at the time of his death on November 27, 1947. He was buried with full military honors at the National Cemetery in Santa Fe, borne to his final resting place by old comrades from his Rough Rider regiment and veterans of the Spanish American and Philippine wars.

Part Three: Stories of Crime & Punishment in Territorial New Mexico

A Scandal Brewing

In late 1885, a social and political scandal was brewing in New Mexico. In the early fall of that year, the *Albuquerque Journal* had reported that a woman convicted of murder in 1884 and sentenced to a one year term in the territorial penitentiary, had recently given birth at approximately the time she had been granted a pardon by Governor Lionel Sheldon. The paper hinted that the woman had been a victim "of the lust of penitentiary guards," and her pardon and release by Governor Sheldon was an attempt to cover-up a political scandal.

Certainly, a pregnant female inmate could have been an embarrassment for the governor and penitentiary officials, but the facts behind this story reveal there was no scandal or cover-up associated with her release. The real story requires a look back at events that began to unfold in early November of 1883 with the reported disappearance of Serafín Candelaria in Albuquerque. Candelaria had last been seen near the home of José Angel Perea in what would be considered Albuquerque's north valley today. Candelaria and Perea had apparently been embroiled in some sort of on-going dispute that was public knowledge, so when Candelaria's body was discovered buried in Perea's vineyard, Perea quickly came under suspicion and was arrested. Perea, however, was soon cleared of any wrongdoing by the confession of Juliana Perea, the eldest of his four daughters.

The reports of her confession are confused and contradictory, but it appears that Juliana, who was married to Francisco Antonio García, had had an earlier relationship with Candelaria. On the night of November 9, 1883, while her father and husband were both absent from the home, Candelaria came to the door in the middle of the night and demanded to be admitted. Juliana and her three sisters were alone in the house and refused to admit Candelaria. When he threatened to break down the door, Juliana warned she would shoot him. Her confession is not clear if he then tried to break into the house or if she shot through the door while Candelaria was still outside, but the following morning, she and her sisters found Candelaria dead behind a wall near the house.

In an attempt to hide the evidence, Juliana and two of her sisters dug a hole in the vineyard, carried Candelaria to the site, tied his hands together "so they didn't have to dig the hole so wide," covered the body with a burlap sack and buried him in his rude grave. Juliana apparently never denied she killed Candelaria, but contended she had shot in fear and self defense and his death was accident. The newspaper reports indicated there was a general feeling that her claim was "a little off the truth," and speculated the pair was having an illicit affair. The paper felt Candelaria had been actually been killed by "parties yet unknown" after being caught in a compromising situation with Juliana.

But Juliana stuck to her story. At the May 1884 term of district court for Bernalillo County, she was indicted for the premeditated murder of Serafín Candelaria. At the subsequent term of court held in October of that year, a jury found her guilty of the lesser charge of fifth-degree murder and was sentenced to one year in the territorial penitentiary in Santa Fe.

The timing of her conviction and sentence to serve a year in the territorial penitentiary makes it difficult to determine for certain where Juliana spent the next several months of her life. In 1884, the new territorial penitentiary was still under construction, so persons convicted in New Mexico's district courts were sent to the Kansas State Prison or served their term in the Santa Fe County jail located on Water Street. Since Juliana was to serve only a one-year term, she probably spent it at the Water Street location in Santa Fe, where she was housed in what the paper described as "an apartment to herself."

It was during her confinement that Juliana's pregnancy came to public attention. The governor's records show that in response to petitions that apparently pointed out her condition, Governor Sheldon pardoned Juliana Perea on May 11, 1885. It was at this point that the *Albuquerque Journal* reported her release under what it considered suspicious circumstances.

The *Santa Fe Weekly Leader*, a rival newspaper, however, advanced an explanation and chided the *Journal* for its hasty and unfounded accusations against recently appointed penitentiary warden James E. Gregg. The *Leader* reported the pregnancy was easily explained. While Juliana was in jail, the paper claimed, her husband frequently paid her what we would today call conjugal visits, and according to the paper, the couple often spent "a half-day in the lady's apartment alone." The *Leader's* story concluded the *Journal* may have injured the "character of this lady," and implied that some type of retraction or apology was in order.

We will never know the whole story behind the killing of Serafín Candelaria and can only speculate what went on in Juliana Perea's jail cell. The public record of their lives, however, serves to remind us that today's soap operas may be tame compared to the dramatic and often sordid realities of society a century ago.

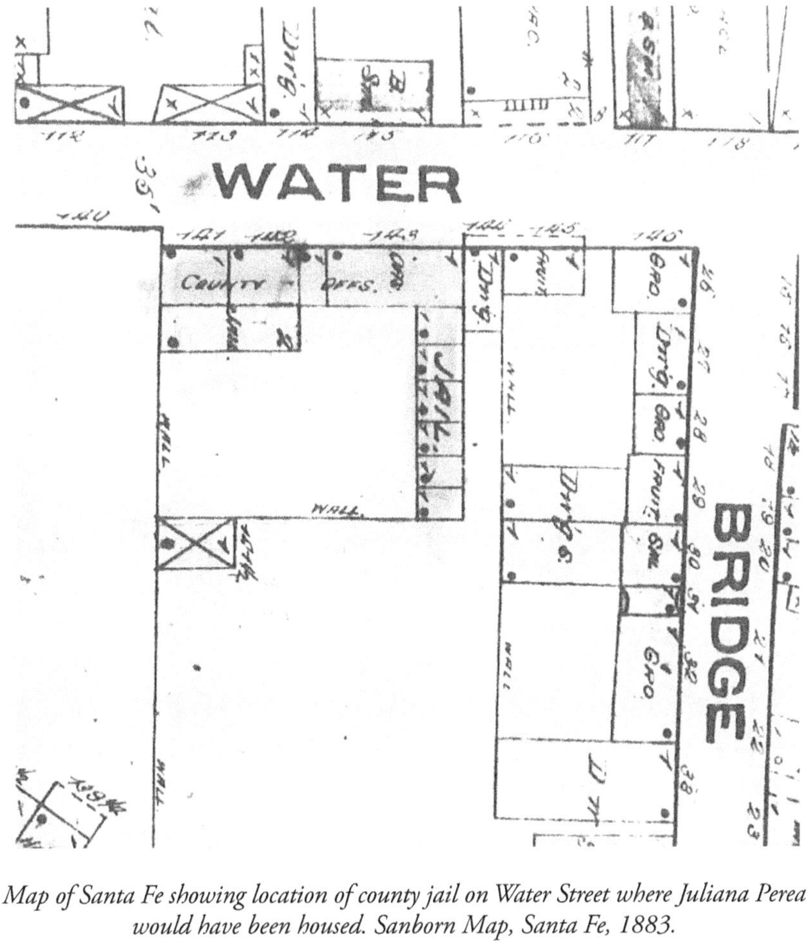

Map of Santa Fe showing location of county jail on Water Street where Juliana Perea would have been housed. Sanborn Map, Santa Fe, 1883.

New Mexico's "Hanging Governor"

The history of crime and punishment in the "wild west" is often associated with the subject of famous outlaws and colorful characters such as Judge Roy Bean and the infamous "hanging judge" Isaac Parker. New Mexico had its share of outlaws who achieved a degree of infamy and many of the best-known characters of that genre come readily to mind. However, most would be hard-pressed to name one New Mexico judge who achieved even a degree of the name recognition of Bean or Parker.

The fame of judges such as Isaac Parker is generally not associated with how good or effective they were as jurists but how many men they sentenced to hang. When one considers that Judge Isaac Parker is credited with hanging more than eighty of the 160 men he sentenced to death, the accomplishments of New Mexico's judiciary pales by comparison. Only two New Mexico judges, Kirby Benedict and Warren Bristol, had careers that marginally qualify them as "hanging judges." Each of these saw six of the men they sentenced to hang actually executed. One reason for this extraordinary difference is that there were "only" fifty-two legal hangings during the entirely of New Mexico's territorial period. It is also important to understand that for most of New Mexico's territorial period, the ultimate decision for the carrying out, or execution of a death sentence imposed by a duly constituted court, fell not to the presiding judge, but to the governor. Until the term of Miguel A. Otero, it was the governor who had the duty and responsibility to issue the actual death warrant to the county sheriff. Ultimately, the governor decided if a death penalty would actually be imposed.

This meant the governor alone decided whether or not to exercise his privilege of executive clemency. Not even the judge in a capital case had any say in the matter. A judge presided over the case, but if a jury returned a verdict of guilty of first- degree murder, the law required that the judge impose a sentence of death by hanging. It was then up to the governor to decide whether it would be carried out. His options for executive clemency included pardon and outright release of a condemned person, but there are only a few examples of such direct pardons. Executive clemency by the governor in capital cases usually consisted of a commutation of the death sentence to one of life imprisonment.

In territorial New Mexico, sixteen separate governors allowed the death penalty to be imposed on fifty-two persons, including one woman. Of these, Governor William Taylor Thornton, who served as governor from 1893-1897, allowed the most. Thirteen men, a quarter of the total number of executions in territorial New Mexico, were hanged during Thornton's term of office.

Governor Thornton's attitude towards capital punishment, and possibly that of society in general at the time, was exemplified by his denial of clemency in one of territorial New Mexico's most celebrated and politically tinged criminal cases – the 1895 conviction and death sentences imposed on four men for the murder of former Santa Fe County Sheriff Francisco Chaves. In his denial of their request for a commutation of their death sentences, Thornton wrote:

> It is time that the criminal classes of the territory should learn that when they deliberately defy the law...they must expect the law to be meted out to them to its fullest extent...When criminals...learn they violate the law at their peril, that justice will surely overtake them...crime will become less frequent, life and property will be safer, and good order and quietude will prevail.

Thornton's seems to have felt there was a close relationship between the need for law and order and strict enforcement of the death penalty. On April 2, 1897, four men, Antonio Gonzales y Borrego, his brother Francisco and their accomplices, Laurino Alarid and Patricio Valencia, were hanged in Santa Fe. These tenth, eleventh, twelfth and thirteenth executions of Governor

Thornton's term apparently weighed heavily on him. That same day, Thornton abruptly submitted his resignation to President William McKinley and left office three days later, April 5, 1897.

On his last day in office, Governor Thornton commuted the sentence of a young man who was in the territorial penitentiary serving a two and a one-half year sentence for assault with a deadly weapon. The eighteen year old convict was named José Gonzales y Borrego. The last official act of New Mexico's "hanging governor" was to pardon the brother of two of the men he had hanged three days earlier.

Death Songs

The *corrido*, or folk ballad, has long been one of the traditional means of conveying news and personal stories. A broad range of ballads tell of important events, adventures, and oftentimes, tragic or bittersweet personal stories. It has been said that these *corridos* were composed almost as soon as an event occurred and were conveyed from town to town by balladeers that traveled from community to community with troupes of *maromeros*. The stanzas of ballads composed to honor prominent individuals who had died were frequently published in local Spanish-language newspapers along with official obituaries.

Some of the most interesting *corridos* are associated with individuals that were awaiting execution after being sentenced to death by a court of law. The oldest reference to one of these "death songs" in New Mexico is the ballad entitled "*El Condenado a Muerte,*" published by Arthur Leon Campa in *Spanish Folk – Poetry in New Mexico*. The author of the poem is unknown, but the text is attributed to Rafael Lucero of El Pino, New Mexico. This *corrido* tells the story of an unnamed individual who was condemned to die on July 20, 1832. However, there is no evidence that the event described in this ballad took place in New Mexico. While it is likely that the *corrido* is genuine, it probably described an event that took place in Mexico and subsequently translated north by troubadours or published in a Spanish-language newspaper.

There are, however, five well-documented *corridos* about individuals awaiting their legal execution. Two of these were authored by the condemned men themselves. The earliest of these was written by Ignacio Montañes, who was executed at San Miguel del Vado on April 11, 1856. The other is by Damian Romero, a teenager hanged at Springer on February 1, 1883. Of these two, the more fascinating is that of Ignacio Montañes.

The extant record suggests that Montañes was a literate and articulate individual. The records of his trial include a poignant final letter to the judge asking for clemency. His "*despedida del mundo*," or farewell to the world, was published in the *Santa Fe Weekly Gazette* the same week he was executed. It consists of thirty five stanzas, in which Montañes admits his guilt, asks for forgiveness, and warns others of the dangers of the life he led. Montañes accepts his fate, thanks the local priest for his consolation and receives the last sacraments of the church. His final appeal for mercy is to God Himself:

Dios verdadero y eterno	True and eternal God
Yo se que tu me recives	I know that you will receive me
Y te pido que me libres	And I ask that you protect me
De las llamas del infierno	From the flames of hell

There are two additional *corridos* of this type. One is about Toribio Huerta, who was executed at Las Cruces in 1901, and the other for Carlos Saiz, executed at Socorro in 1907. The authors of these two are unknown but John Donald Robb, in his *Hispanic Folk Music of New Mexico and the Southwest*, attributes the Huerta text to José Faquis of Tijeras and the Saiz *corrido* to M. A. Esquibel of Las Nutrias. Both of these *corridos* follow a standard format of verses consisting of four lines each. Each tells the story of the crime and attempts to caution others from following the same "path to perdition." What is most fascinating about the Saiz *corrido* is that the last words attributed to him in the ballad correspond closely to those reported in news stories of his execution. His last words included a warning to the youth about their choice of friends:

No lleguen a esta ocación	Do not arrive at this occasion
Esto me sucedió a mi	This happened to me
Por un amigo traidor	Because of a traitorous friend

The fifth death song is that of Paula Angel, the only woman executed in territorial New Mexico. What we know about Paula Angel is told in a chapter devoted to her in my book, *Myth of the Hanging Tree*, published by the

University of New Mexico Press in 2008, and will not be retold here except to note that Paula was hanged at Las Vegas in 1861. The ballad of her life and tragic end was first brought to public attention by the research of Julián Josué Vigil, who has published several accounts of the poem. According to Vigil, "*La Homicida Paula*" was authored by Juan Angel, Paula's cousin. The stanzas of his poem closely follow the account left us by a scant historical record. It tells a poignant story of the burden of her condemnation, an appeal for forgiveness and bewilderment at what she has been through:

¡Hay, desgraciada Pablita!	Oh wretched Pablita!
¿Que es lo que te ha susedido?	What has happened to you?

One can easily imagine these ballads being spread by troubadours throughout the territory as they traveled from village to village, literally bringing the latest and juiciest news to a populace eager to be informed and entertained. These *corridos* also served to warn others of the fate that awaited those who did not conform to the laws of man and God.

A Cruel and Unusual Punishment

One of the most common forms of corporal punishment imposed by courts of law throughout history has been whipping. It may have been called by other names, but the act of inflicting, or "laying on" of lashes on the back or other parts of the human body has been around for centuries. In New Mexico, the Spanish colonial judicial system often imposed public floggings on those convicted of theft or other petty crimes. New Mexico's judicial records from the Spanish through Territorial periods, contain numerous cases that show the circumstances under which the law allowed the use of lashes (*azotes*) as well as examples of how the punishment was imposed in individual cases.

One of the best examples on how whipping was used in New Mexico is from a 1768 *bando*, or edict, from Governor Fermín Mendinueta regarding the persistent theft of produce from gardens and fields. The order indicated that any man, woman, or child found with stolen produce, or in the act of stealing "any type of fruits of the earth," would be punished by being tied to a pillory (*picota*), or pole. If the individual was of *color quebrado*, or mixed blood, the punishment was twenty five lashes inflicted while the culprit was tied to the pillory. If the thief was a white person, or *español*, he or she would be spared the lashes, but was to be tied to the pole and publicly humiliated by having the stolen produce draped around their neck.

The Spanish government abolished whipping as punishment in 1813, a concession extended to Indians the following year. Whipping, however, was reintroduced to New Mexico by the Kearny Code in 1846. These new

American statutes listed several criminal offenses that were to be punished by "stripes well laid on," usually to the bare back. Robbery or burglary, for example, carried sentences of imprisonment for up to ten years, along with thirty-nine lashes. The significance of this odd number is uncertain, but may be attributed to 2 Corinthians 11:24, "Of the Jews five times did I receive forty stripes save one." Larceny and theft also carried varying degrees of imprisonment and lashes ranging in number from twenty to one hundred.

Early New Mexico district court records show the punishment was imposed often and severely. During the March 1847 term of court in Santa Fe, one witness noted an individual convicted of perjury was tied [probably on the plaza] "hugging the flag staff and receiving… 65 lashes on his naked hide." During this same term of court, Miguel Molina was convicted of larceny and sentenced to "fifty lashes on his bare back well laid on." Twenty five of the lashes were inflicted within fifteen minutes of when the sentence was imposed and the remaining twenty five the following morning. Molina was also remitted to prison until he paid the costs of prosecution. Similar sentences are found in numerous court records for a number of years.

This early territorial law did not distinguish between men and women. While I have not found examples of women sentenced to be whipped, this detail of the law was corrected in 1853 by the territorial legislature when it specifically exempted women from "stripes" and replaced the punishment with a form of domestic service in "private homes" for periods ranging from six months to two years.

Whipping as punishment was not universally accepted in New Mexico. In his message to the legislature in December 1866, acting Governor William F. M. Arny recommended the law be repealed. He called the practice "a barbarous custom" and suggested it be replaced with sentences "more in consonance with civilization." The law was also challenged by some individuals upon whom it was imposed by the courts. In 1868 Nestor García was indicted and convicted of larceny in the theft of a mule valued at two hundred dollars. Garcia appealed the conviction and sentence to the Territorial Supreme Court, claiming the punishment was unconstitutional because it constituted "cruel and unusual punishment" prohibited by article eight of the U. S. Constitution.

The opinion of the higher court, as written by Justice C. J. Watts, rejected the appeal. It noted that whipping had been in common and wide use, and that the word "cruel" in the constitution was not intended to "abridge or limit the selection by the law-making power of such punishment as was deemed most effective in the punishment and suppression of crime." As such, the court would not hinder the territory's ability to effectively punish its "vicious and lawless" citizens. The court ordered the sentence be carried out as imposed by the lower court.

In 1870, the territorial legislature abolished whipping and the imposition of lashes as punishment for convicted criminals in New Mexico and replaced it with a series of fines and imprisonment in county jails for terms ranging from one month to five years. When this remnant of the Kearny Code was repealed, it ended more than two centuries of this cruel, but tragically, not so unusual punishment in New Mexico.

"My Dear Darling Husband"

As I browsed through the pardon papers of Governor L. Bradford Prince (1889-1893) in the Territorial Archives of New Mexico, my attention was drawn to a letter that opened, "My Dear Darling Husband." The letter caught my eye because it was unusual to find such a personal and affectionate greeting among the correspondence of convicts seeking executive clemency from the governor.

The letter, dated November 12, 1888, was written by Emma L. Johnson to her husband, Otter Johnson, Penitentiary of New Mexico inmate No. 291, who was serving a three year sentence at the territorial penitentiary for third degree murder. "I send you a few lines to help you to bear your present trials," Mrs. Johnson wrote. She assured her husband that "this trouble has endeared you to me more than I can tell you..." and playfully chided Johnson about picking up bad habits in prison. "Now Darling, don't spoil your sweet mouth by learning to smoke," she wrote, "remember I want you just as you went away."

The file also contains a letter from Mattie, Johnson's thirteen year old daughter. The teenager wrote to her "Dear Papa" shortly after Christmas, 1888, and told him about a Christmas party at the Presbyterian Church. A Christmas tree was on display and all the children had received "candies, nuts, fruits and Christmas Cards." They also had an entertaining program in which Mattie had a speaking part. She wished her father a "Happy Christmas" and asked that he keep up his spirits, predicting that "the time will fly by" and he would be back home.

What a wonderful story this will make, I thought. Here we have correspondence showing a family that was able to maintain an affectionate and supportive relationship under the most trying circumstances. But it was too good to be true! Sometime between those late 1888 letters and the year that followed, Otter and Emma Johnson's world fell apart.

In a December 14, 1889 letter to Governor Prince, Johnson asked for executive clemency and an early release because he received information that Emma had "commenced using liquor very much" and was keeping bad company. She had filed for a divorce and Johnson was concerned for his daughter's well being and hoped an early release would enable him save his daughter "from ruin."

Governor Prince apparently took a serious look at Johnson's petition for clemency and contacted various individuals in southwest New Mexico for information. The responses from Silver City and Lordsburg, however, were mixed. Idus and James Fielder, who had defended Johnson at his trial, felt strongly that Johnson's killing of Norman Buck was a clear case of self-defense and that their client had been unjustly convicted. J. M. Ashenfelter, the Grant County District Attorney who had prosecuted the case, felt otherwise and informed Prince that Johnson did not deserve leniency and that many people locally felt Johnson "should have been hung."

Things got worse. On July 9, 1890, the Fielder brothers informed Johnson that Emma had recently died and provided some troubling details of her estrangement from Johnson and the deteriorating physical and mental state that apparently led to her death. They tried to console their former client, suggesting he had "little if any *real* cause for regret at her death," noting she "was completely alienated from you and …she grew more and more indifferent, and this indifference gravitated into unfriendliness and finally into positive opposition and hatred." To make things worse, Emma also seems to have alienated Mattie from her father. When the Fielders circulated a petition in support of Johnson's pardon, they approached Mattie for help, but she refused. "No Sir," she allegedly informed them, "I will not take [the petition] around, I don't want anything to do with Papa."

Mattie Johnson's disregard for her father is quite evident in a letter she wrote to Governor Prince on July 19, 1890. She had learned from the local post master that the governor was inquiring about her situation and that Otter Johnson was concerned that J. P. Ownby, who had been appointed executor for Emma's estate, was an inappropriate guardian for the young girl. In her letter, Mattie advised Prince that when her father had gone to the penitentiary, Emma had willed everything to her and had left enough for her education and care. She assured the governor that Ownby was a good man and expressed confidence that he was an honest executor. The letter does not mention her father in any way.

Mattie's confident letter must have assured Governor Prince that Mattie was in no danger of "ruin" and he set aside Johnson's appeal for clemency for nearly a year. On July 23, 1891, Prince finally issued a pardon and ordered Johnson's release a mere six months before his three year sentence was set to expire. One can only wonder whether Otter Johnson recalled the hopeful and affectionate words Emma had written to him less than three years earlier and whether he had anything to look forward to as he stepped through the penitentiary gates that summer of 1891.

A Rough Week in Santa Fe

Violence along the frontier is a common theme in stories about the West. A notion of the "wild west" seems to revolve around disputes and shootouts; desperate men doing dastardly deeds and forces of the law attempting to right them. It is often difficult to think of Santa Fe, New Mexico's capitol city, as part of this western milieu. We think of the ancient *villa* and capital as a civilized seat of government and center of commerce. A look through Santa Fe's territorial-period newspapers, however, belies this image. Such was the week of April 5 through April 12, 1880. A cursory review of the Santa Fe *Weekly New Mexican* for that period reveals enough "wild west" moments to show that the capital city was not immune to the violence that plagued so many western communities. The crimes reported that week included a threat with a shotgun, cases of fraud, a stabbing, the murder of a stage driver near present-day Española, and a fatal shoot-out near the plaza in Santa Fe.

Early the morning of April 5, Hawkins' saloon, located in the old Theatre Comique on San Francisco Street, was the site of a confrontation in which James Dugan was stabbed and seriously injured by a man identified as A. Schumaker. Dugan was asleep on a table in the saloon when Schumaker entered the saloon, and as a joke, shook Dugan awoke. Dugan, likely nursing a hangover, apparently did not appreciate Shumaker's humor, drew a pocket knife and took a small slice off one of Schumaker's ears. In retaliation, Schumaker drew a "dirk," a long straight bladed dagger, from his pocket and stabbed Dugan twice, once in the neck and once in the abdomen. Schumaker then calmly walked out the door and made his escape without interference from any of the witnesses.

The newspaper felt this incident was especially galling because one of the witnesses to the whole affair was Charles Wheeler, a city constable who did not stop the fight or hinder Schumaker's escape. Wheeler was apparently present when the argument started but did nothing except tell the two men to keep quiet when he was asked by the bartender to do something before the fight escalated. According to witnesses, when Dugan was stabbed, Carpenter "took to his heels," and went outside "blowing his whistle valiantly for assistance … too careful of his own precious skin to make an effort to stop [Schumaker]." Most of the story was a tirade against Wheeler, who was described as "a coward…unworthy to wear the badge of an officer of the law."

Newspaper reports do not elaborate further on this crime but violence continued to swirl around Hawkins' saloon that week. Shortly after midnight, April 12, 1880, William T. Robinson, a shoemaker who had been drinking heavily, entered the Hawkins' establishment carrying a large "cap and ball" .44 caliber revolver in his pocket. Robinson sat silently at a table for a while then exited the saloon. Earlier that day, Robinson had severely beaten the woman with whom he was living and drove her out of the house. He seems to have been a deeply troubled individual who would have been easily provoked into more violence. One report even characterized him as professional "bad man." Whatever that report meant, Robinson did seem to be looking for a fight. Unfortunately for him, he ended up choosing the wrong opponent.

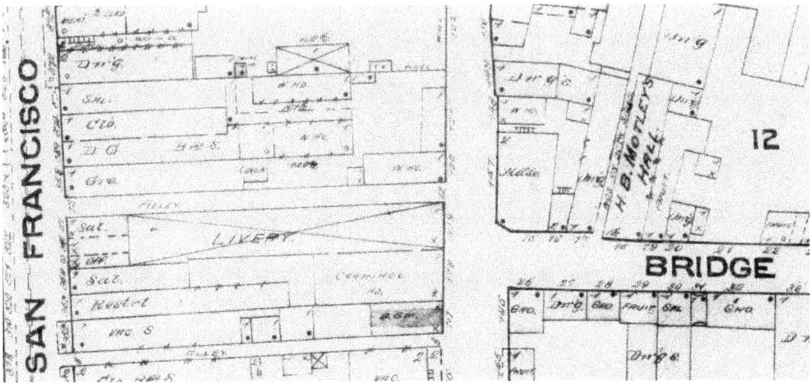

Motley's saloon near the corner of Bridge and Water streets is prominently featured in the 1883 Sanborn Insurance map of Santa Fe.

That night a local policeman identified only as "Officer Sunday" was patrolling the streets of Santa Fe when a single gunshot rang out. Sunday proceeded to investigate the source and walked south along an alley leading from San Francisco Street in the direction of Mottley's Theatre. Unable to find anyone who could have fired the gunshot, Sunday continued walking towards the river. As he neared the creek, Robinson approached him on the opposite side of the street. Suddenly, as the two men walked past each other, Robinson halted, drew his revolver and shouted at Sunday, "You son of a bitch, you might as well get this as anyone," and fired twice in quick succession. The first ball struck Sunday on the third finger of the right hand. "Hold on you fool! I am a policeman," he shouted as the second shot rang out, hitting Sunday again on the same hand. With his right hand disabled, Sunday drew his own Colt .45 with his left hand and fired once, striking his assailant squarely in the chest. Robinson discharged his revolver a third time as he fell forward, mortally wounded.

The whole affair lasted only a few seconds while the men stood on opposite sides of a dark street a mere thirty feet apart. A coroner's jury ruled that Sunday had acted in self defense and in the "discharge of his duty" as a police officer. No glory or fanfare, just an unexplained, brief, and deadly eruption of gunfire in the middle of the night, ending another violent episode in New Mexico's "wild west" period.

The New Mexico Boys School

The New Mexico Boys School in Springer was closed in 2006, bringing an ignominious end to an institution that served New Mexico's youth for nearly a century. At the time it closed, the Boys School, or as it was often referred to, the "Reform School," was one of the oldest governmental institutions in the state.

The New Mexico Reform School, as it was known for several decades, was established by the territorial legislature in 1903. This school for New Mexico's "wayward" youth was originally intended to be in the northern Rio Arriba County community of El Rito. However, for a number of reasons that are not entirely clear, it never opened at this location, and in 1909, the territorial legislature decided to move the reform school from El Rito and relocated it to northeast community of Springer in Colfax County. At the same legislative session, lawmakers created the Spanish American Normal School and decided to house the school in the building at El Rito that had been originally intended for the reform school. The reform school officially opened in Springer on October 1, 1909 in the building and grounds that constituted the old Colfax County Courthouse and jail. The venerable old building still stands today and is the site of an excellent locally managed museum.

One can only imagine what condition the old building was in when the young inmates occupied the facility. One of the first annual reports by school officials indicated they had completed significant repairs and remodeling that first year. New floors, windows and doors were installed, a stone wall around the property was partially rebuilt and an adjacent brick building was purchased from the Mills Ranch Resort Company and renovated for use as a classroom. Most of the work was reportedly done by the student inmates themselves.

The New Mexico Reform School at Springer, New Mexico. Robert J. Tórrez Collection.

One early improvement of note was a bathing pool in a room that included a one hundred gallon hot water storage tank that also provided hot water for the laundry. The June 30, 1911 report by Superintendent Jonathon Kirkpatrick expressed great pride in this accomplishment. Previously, the institution's bathing facility consisted of one small bath tub in which it took up to a day and a half for all the boys to bathe (the report did not specify how often they bathed). Now, everyone could bathe in two hours.

These early reports emphasize the school's farm operations on the hundred acres they had under cultivation. Up to fifty acres were planted with beans and the balance with alfalfa and other forage crops. The superintendent was especially proud of a three acre garden in which they grew cabbage, lettuce, spinach, peas, turnips, cauliflower, radishes and other vegetables. Superintendent Kirkpatrick felt they not only had the "finest garden in northern New Mexico," but boasted that the produce contributed substantially to healthy meals for the boys and reduced the cost of operating the institution.

The earliest extant list of the boys and young men at the reform school is from early 1912. The diverse population consisted of fifty- six inmates from twenty four separate New Mexico communities. Albuquerque, with eight, had the most referrals, with Alamogordo, Las Vegas and Silver City, three each. The list also shows inmates that came from nine other states and one from Canada.

The oldest inmate was twenty one years of age and the youngest were two nine year old boys. More than half of them, however, were sixteen and seventeen. Eighteen of the young men were Spanish surnamed and thirty eight were non- Spanish surnamed. The later may have included one Native American whose tribal affiliation is not listed.

The school's early years were not without growing pains. In September 1910 three inmates assaulted the assistant superintendent in an apparent escape attempt. The culprits were captured, indicted by a grand jury, and in an example of the swift justice of the time, quickly sentenced to penitentiary terms. The school also had ongoing problems with funding and certain "non-essential services" such as education were periodically cut or eliminated as a result. Funding issues also caused problems with sanitation, a serious issue investigated by Captain Fred Fornoff of the New Mexico Mounted Police in 1912. Fornoff's report included a recommendation for a one thousand foot sewer line to channel the school's sewage into the nearby river.

By 1915, the school's annual reports show concern over a growing inmate population that could no longer be properly housed in the old courthouse building. This naturally led to recommendations for a new building and expansion of programs for education and industrial training that evolved into the now closed institution. The young men of today's world would probably be appalled at the thought of working on a school farm to produce their own food and mending their own clothing; in retrospect, however, the inmate of a century ago would not recognize the facilities and opportunities made available today.

The Penitentiary of New Mexico's First "Mug Shot"

There are many documentary treasures at the New Mexico State Records Center and Archives in Santa Fe. One of my personal favorites is the collection of Penitentiary of New Mexico records that document the original (and now demolished) penitentiary from the day it opened in 1885. This archive includes a wonderful collection of glass plate negatives of inmate "mug shots" beginning with inmate # 637. It is possible the penitentiary began to photograph inmates before this, but if the practice began earlier than the day this individual was accepted at the penitentiary on April 28, 1893, the negatives taken before this date have disappeared. I imagine the tragic moment when someone stumbled and dropped a box of the fragile glass negatives, shattering the pictorial record of earlier inmates. Even worse, one can imagine the decision of some bureaucrat to dispose of these irreplaceable images from the past because they were taking up space and would be of no possible interest or value to anyone.

Nevertheless, many of them did survive, and the earliest of these shows the image of inmate #637, a man named José D. Gallegos. The photograph shows a husky, sullen, angry man. Gallegos had every reason to glare at the camera. When the mug shot was taken after Gallegos entered the penitentiary on April 28, 1893, all he had to look forward to was a very long stretch of incarnation – on that day, he began serving a life sentence for murder.

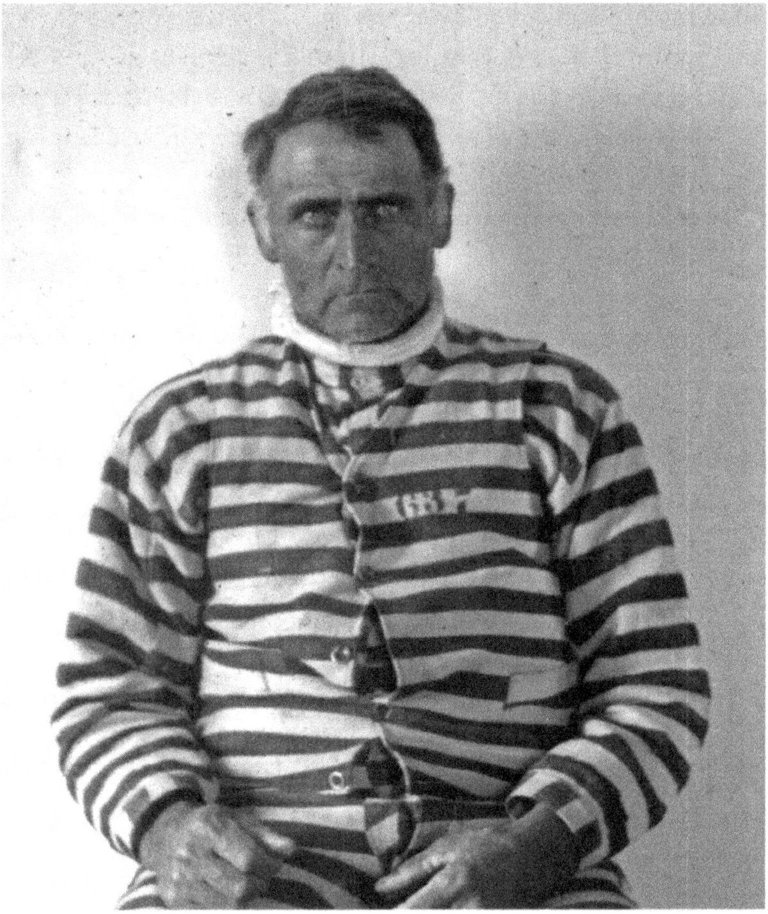

Jose M. Gallegos, PNM #637. New Mexico Dept. of Corrections, 1970-006, Convict Photographs, New Mexico . State Records Center and Archives.

The story of José D. Gallegos' imprisonment begins with the murder of John J. Schmidt, a Wagon Mound merchant, on July 1, 1892. The formal language of the indictment tells us that on that day, Gallegos, "…with premeditated malice and malice aforethought deliberately…did shoot…him the said John Justus Schmidt…in and upon the left breast, and in and upon the right shoulder…of which mortal wounds the said [Schmidt] then and there died."

Newspaper reports of the incident indicate the shooting took place in a field north of Wagon Mound while that part of northeast New Mexico was still part of Mora County. The details of what happened are skimpy, but the pair allegedly had a disagreement over some sheep Gallegos had on shares. Schmidt apparently accused Gallegos of stealing some of the sheep and in the ensuing argument, exchanged gunfire. Schmidt was shot twice but managed to kill Gallegos' horse and wound him in the left leg before he died. Gallegos made his escape on foot.

Law enforcement officers quickly mounted a search for Gallegos. The search parties included a deputy sheriff from Trinidad, Colorado, who brought two blood hounds that managed to follow his trail into the mountains. The posse, however, was unable to find Gallegos, and on July 4, Governor L. Bradford Prince issued a reward offer of two hundred dollars for his arrest and delivery to the Mora County Sheriff. Fearing rumors of a lynching, Gallegos surrendered himself to San Miguel County Sheriff Lorenzo López a few days later.

Gallegos was indicted for murder by a Mora County grand jury on October 22, 1892. The trial, however, was delayed for several months because Gallegos' attorney immediately filed a motion for a change of venue. His petition noted that Schmidt "was a prominent citizen...and well known in both the counties of Mora and Colfax," and that the murder had "caused great public excitement against the defendant" in those counties. The court agreed Gallegos could probably not get a fair trial in either county and allowed a change of venue to San Miguel.

Gallegos' trial was held during the April 1993 term of court for San Miguel County at Las Vegas. At the trial, Gallegos asserted that the shooting was justifiable because Schmidt had shot at him first. But he was unable to prove the assertion in court, and on April 27, 1893, the jury returned a verdict of guilty in the second degree. Gallegos was sentenced to life imprisonment in the territorial penitentiary. If he had been found guilty in the first degree, territorial law carried a mandatory sentence of death by hanging.

Upon his arrival at the penitentiary, José D. Gallegos became inmate #637, the subject of our "first mug shot." The intake information shows he was 44 years old, a "stock raiser" born in Las Vegas, married with four children. His personal description confirms that he was a big man, five feet, eleven inches tall and weighed just over 180 pounds. It also shows he had a good education, having attained some college. Maybe he was a graduate of the Jesuit college at Las Vegas or St. Michael's in Santa Fe.

The official record tells us little more about Gallegos. The final entry in his penitentiary records shows only that on March 10, 1901, he died in prison of unstated causes. He had served less than seven years, yet, for José D. Gallegos, Penitentiary of New Mexico inmate # 637, it had, indeed been a life sentence.

"to see the cars jump"

On June 11, 1892, *The Daily New Mexican* printed a small item under the title "Mischief Makers." The paper reported that the passenger train had been derailed about two miles south of Santa Fe early that afternoon. The engine, baggage car and two passenger coaches had left the track, leaving the passengers "pretty well shaken up" but only a few minor injuries were reported. The passengers and mail were brought in by carriage and a crew was sent to deal with the derailed train. The same report indicated the derailment had been caused by some spikes or bolts someone had driven into the ties along the rails. Suspicion fell on two students from the United States Indian School who were caught near the scene of the incident.

Two days later the paper reported that two Indian School students from the San Carlos Apache Reservation, Rob Roy and David Owanda had been arrested. The paper, citing what it called "the natural vein of cussedness that characterizes the San Carlos Apache," indicated the boys had admitted they had driven spikes in the rails simply because they wanted "to see the cars jump." The boys, whose age was estimated at about 17, were placed in the city jail to await action by a grand jury.

Rob Roy and David Owanda, who was also known as David Owen, were in serious trouble. Derailing a train was a major felony. In territorial New Mexico, it was the only crime other that first-degree murder that carried a death sentence. Fortunately for the boys, the statute also allowed a lesser sentence of three years in the penitentiary at the discretion of the judge.

On June 14, 1892, a Santa Fe County grand jury issued the following indictment for both boys:

> [That Rob Roy and David Owen alias David Owanda] did unlawfully, willfully, maliciously, and feloniously, put and place a piece of iron, the said piece of iron then and there being an obstruction, upon the New Mexico and Southern Pacific Railroad Company's railroad track in the county of Santa Fe… for the purpose and with the intent then and there to throw the locomotive and railroad cars…from the said railroad track, contrary to the form of the statute in such case made and provided, and against the peace and dignity of the territory of New Mexico.

But there was no trial. In a plea bargain that may have been reached to avoid a jury trial that could have resulted in a conviction and death sentence, the boys pleaded guilty and were quickly sentenced to the minimum three years allowed by statute. Interestingly, the boys were admitted to the penitentiary on June 14, 1892. That means the grand jury indictment, the guilty plea, sentencing, and imprisonment all took place on the same day!

The Penitentiary of New Mexico "Description of Convicts" paints a pathetic image of the boys that would be unimaginable today. As they entered the penitentiary gates, they became inmates #568 (Rob Roy) and #569 (David Owanda). As it turns out, they were much younger than initially reported. Rob was only 12 and David, 15; they were tiny by any standard of the day; Rob was less that 4'11" tall and weighed 95 pounds; David was scarcely an inch taller and also weighed 95 pounds. Both boys showed scaring and tattoos that may have been ceremonial tribal markings. There is no indication the boys were housed separate from the general convict population.

The official record shows nothing about Rob and David until late February 1893 when Indian School superintendent S. M. Cash inquired about the boys. Penitentiary superintendent Jonathon R. DeMier advised Cash that their conduct "has been near perfect…never having been punished or reprimanded." By early March, several petitions for their pardon and release were submitted to Governor L. Bradford Prince. One of the petitions noted the boys had never seen a train until they came to school in Santa Fe and blamed their actions on age and youthful ignorance. Even Judge Edward Seeds, who had sentenced the boys, joined the campaign for their freedom. Judge Seeds indicated the boys deserved punishment for what they did, but even at that time, he felt the minimum sentence of three years was too harsh "considering their age and knowledge." He felt they had been sufficiently punished and recommend executive clemency.

That was all Governor Prince needed to hear. Citing the petitions for clemency from "numerous prominent citizens" and Judge Seeds' conclusion that three years imprisonment was too harsh, he commuted their sentence to one year. With an additional month apparently taken off the sentence for good behavior, both boys were released from the penitentiary on May 11, 1893. They had served little less than one year for their youthful indiscretion. One wonders if they felt the momentary excitement of "seeing the cars jump" had been worth it.

Ada Humes, "A Murderess in Clover"

Among the countless stories contained in New Mexico's vast array of historical records are those of the many fascinating characters that we learn about because they managed to get in trouble with the law. Among these is a captivating personality named Ada Humes. We know quite a bit (but not the whole story) about Ada because she killed a man in Silver City the evening of February 19, 1889. The newspaper reports, court proceedings and penitentiary records of the time provide us a glimpse of a woman who must have lived a tragic, but nonetheless, interesting life.

Ada Humes was described by the Silver City *Enterprise* as a "good looking, well-developed young woman of 30 years, with a bright and intelligent countenance..." Sometime before 1889, she was abandoned by her husband and left with a young daughter to raise, and took jobs as a piano player in Silver City saloons to support herself. She eventually developed what may have been an abusive relationship with a lover named Jack V. Brown and on the night of the murder, Brown sent Ada a note breaking up the relationship. According to newspaper accounts, Ada tucked a pistol into "the bosom of her dress," walked into the Centennial saloon where Brown was watching a game of cards and shot him to death.

Ada's trial was held on October 1, 1889 at Las Cruces in Doña Ana County on a change of venue from Grant County. Charged with murder, Ada could have been sentenced to death by hanging if the jury determined she was guilty of first-degree murder. Idus Fiedler, her defense attorney, pleaded a combination of self-defense and insanity. He even resorted to a tactic we often see today, justifying the crime by attacking the victim's character. He drew the jury's attention to the "book of Jack Brown's life," in which unfolded the story of a man who had many secrets "stored in the dark arsenal of his lawless life." Fiedler's closing arguments must have had an effect on the jury. On October 4, 1889, they found Ada "guilty of murder in the third degree" and assessed her sentence at three years in the territorial penitentiary, the minimum allowed by law.

The next chapter of Ada's life began when she was admitted to the territorial penitentiary in Santa Fe on October 30, 1889. Her personal information in the "Record of Convicts" suggests she may have been the attractive woman described in the earlier Silver City newspaper. The entries indicate she was 30 years old, with a light complexion, blue eyes, brown hair, divorced, with one child, and her occupation as piano player. Whatever it was about her that stirred strong passions in those she met quickly came into play. Within six weeks of her admission at the penitentiary, a letter from an anonymous writer identified only as "A Visitor" was published in the Las Vegas *Optic* under the title, "A Murderess in Clover." The letter charged prison officials had placed Ada in "one of the best rooms in the penitentiary" instead of a cell and that she spent her days in an adjoining parlor reading, crocheting, or playing a piano. Prison officials, of course, denied they had provided Ada any special treatment, but the following year, her case received more public attention when she petitioned Governor L. Bradford Prince for a pardon.

In a series of letters dated from December 1890 through early 1891, Ada's application for a pardon also invited the governor to visit her at the penitentiary so she could personally plead her case. Governor Prince declined her invitation, but apparently sent Mary E. Teals of the Women's Christian Temperance League to interview Ada. Miss Teals was thoroughly shocked when she met Ada, as her letter to Governor Prince indicates:

> [I am] compelled candidly to say, that she merits very little clemency or consideration...She has no higher aspirations than to go back to her wicked former life...She possesses no small degree of <u>power</u>, in certain directions and <u>she will</u> (underlining by Miss Teals) use it to its fullest extent!

However vague Miss Teals' words are, their meaning is seems clear. Ada had a way of getting what she wanted and had become a "contamination" at the penitentiary. Miss Teals hinted that two unnamed prison officers were taking advantage of the situation. A few weeks later, the warden was fired and replaced by J. Francisco Chaves. Chaves confirmed Ada had been granted some unspecified privileges that were "a gross violation of order and good discipline." He was, however, concerned about what he perceived as Ada's deteriorating mental and physical condition and authorized a series of examinations that produced some fascinating reports of her mental status. One doctor diagnosed her as a "nymphomaniac" in danger of becoming a "raving maniac" without hope of recovery if not released to seek proper care.

These reports convinced Governor Prince that Ada was deserving of executive clemency and he issued her a "full pardon" on June 29, 1891. The official record does not tell us what became of Ada after she was released from the penitentiary and one cannot help but wonder what became of her. Was she truly mentally and physically ill, or did she use her "power" to put one over on the examining physicians and penitentiary officials? Did she return to her "former wicked life," or maybe, as we hope, received proper care, got better, and went on to live a long and fruitful life?

Nicolás Aragón

In 2007, after I had concluded a presentation to the Daughters of the American Revolution in Roswell, Mrs. Laura C. Nelson approached me and related a story about her great uncle, Jasper Corn, who had been killed while in pursuit of outlaws during New Mexico's "wild west" period. As I researched the story, I found that Mrs. Nelson's great uncle was in fact killed as she had recalled. The Territorial Archives of New Mexico show that on November 1, 1884, Governor Lionel Sheldon issued a reward proclamation of $500 for the capture of one Nicolás Aragón for the murder of Jasper N. Corn, a Lincoln County deputy sheriff. It was at this point that my curiosity was diverted from Deputy Sheriff Corn to Aragón, who apparently had quite an eventful, if lawless career.

In May of 1884, Nicolás Aragón and José de la Cruz Tafoya were indicted by a Lincoln County grand jury for stealing horses from Manuel Sisneros, Luciano Trujillo and George Kimbrell. Tafoya pled guilty to one of the charges and was sentenced to four years in the territorial penitentiary. Aragón pleaded "not guilty" but was convicted at trial and sentenced to five years. However, on May 24, 1884, while awaiting transport to the new territorial prison being built in Santa Fe, Aragón escaped from the Lincoln County jail. On November 1, 1884, Governor Sheldon issued a reward proclamation of $200 for his "capture and delivery" to the Lincoln County Sheriff.

In late October 1884, Lincoln County Sheriff John W. Poe received information that Aragón was "holed up" at Gallinas Springs, about thirty miles south of Las Vegas not far from Chaperito. Details on Aragón's encounter with

Deputy Sheriff Jasper Corn and the posse sent to capture him are sketchy, but Corn was killed during an exchange of gunfire. Some suggest Corn was ambushed but others say the posse fired at Aragón first and without warning. Either way, Aragón made his escape and remained at large until after Governor Sheldon issued a second reward proclamation of $500 for his capture.

In late January 1885, Sheriff Poe learned that Aragón had been seen at Chaperito and sent a strong posse to seek him out. On January 27, the posse cornered Aragón at his home and after an extended standoff and exchange of gunfire in which Deputy John Hurley was killed, Aragón was finally talked into surrendering by San Miguel County Sheriff Hilario Romero.

In March 1885, Aragón was indicted by a San Miguel County grand jury for the murders of Corn and Hurley. A change of venue transferred the trials to Santa Fe County, where Aragón faced the first of two trials at the July term of District Court. Aragón was tried for the Hurley murder first, and to everyone's astonishment, he was acquitted!

The *Daily New Mexican* story on the trial suggested that since the shot that killed Hurley was fired in the dark and no one actually saw Aragón fire the fatal shot, the jury decided to give him the benefit of the doubt. The prosecution was stunned by the verdict and immediately filed a motion for a change of venue for the second trial. Their affidavit indicated they could not "have a fair and impartial trial [in Santa Fe]...because upon the trial of the first case against the said defendant...such a strong feeling was created *in his favor* that it would be impossible to obtain a jury...that...could try the case according to law and the evidence..."

Aragón's second trial (for the murder of Jasper Corn) was held in Colfax County, at the September 1885 term of court. This time, the prosecution seemed to have found the venue they were looking for, and the Colfax County jury quickly returned a verdict of guilty. Aragón was sentenced to life imprisonment in the territorial penitentiary but would serve only eleven years of his life sentence. In late November, 1889, his father submitted a petition with more than five pages of signatures, asking for executive clemency. The petition suggested that while "he was incarcerated, [Aragón] has behaved himself in an upright manner and been...active and obedient to his commanders, and has also promised that hereafter he will behave himself in a gentlemanly manner...and [if released] will attend to the due support of his aged father, wife and children."

Over the next four years, Governor L. Bradford Prince sought and collected information about Aragón but received a mixed response. William A. Vincent, an attorney from Las Vegas, felt that the evidence "justified the infliction of the death penalty." Finally, on April 3, 1893, Prince commuted his sentence to twenty years, and with "good time" allowed, Aragón was discharged from the penitentiary on December 24, 1896.

The official record is silent on Aragón's life after his release. At the time of his arrest, stories circulated that "he was an old time killer" with a dozen murders to his credit, and even that he rode with "Billy the Kid's" gang. None of this was ever substantiated, but clearly, he did kill two lawmen while they attempted to do their lawful duty. For that, he served a little more than eleven years of incarceration. Whether or not justice was done may be a matter of debate, but in retrospect, we can hope that Nicolás Aragón did in fact "go straight" and fulfilled the promise made in his father's petition for his release.

A Chicago Gangster

When I was growing up in the northern New Mexico village of Los Ojos, my paternal grandmother Silveria used to tell us stories about "El Looney," who she describe as "*un gangster de Chicago.*" I do not recall specifics she told us about the man, only that he had a large ranch in western Rio Arriba County near Stinking Lake adjacent to the Jicarilla Apache Reservation. He was apparently a wanted man "back east" and used his New Mexico ranch as a hideout. I always wondered how his ranch could be much of a hideout if his ownership was public knowledge and everyone seemed to know who he was, but like most stories told to us by the *viejitos* (elders), we simply enjoyed them without being too concerned whether or not they were true. One also has to consider that until quite recently, that part of northern New Mexico is not easily accessible.

As it turns out, there really was a "Chicago gangster" that hid out in Rio Arriba. His name was John Looney. The 1920 census lists him as a "farmer" in the El Vado precinct of Rio Arriba County. That same year, Looney is listed in the New Mexico Business Directory as a "wool grower." To most residents, he seemed to be just another large ranch owner, raising sheep and cattle on his 30,000 acre spread. The late Art Daggett, who wrote local interest stories for *The Nora News*, a popular monthly published by the local electric cooperative in Chama for many years, knew Looney personally and described him as "...a gentleman...It was hard to believe he was an outlaw."

But Looney was a wanted man. He had been a "power in politics" in Rock Island, Illinois, a city located along the Illinois-Iowa border west of

Chicago. He came to New Mexico sometime before 1920 to avoid prosecution for murder and other charges. When Looney returned to Rock Island in 1921 he was implicated in the murder of a witness in a corruption case that had been developed against him.

John P. Looney reward poster. Rock Island (Illinois) Historical Society.

In October 1922, a United States federal grand jury also indicted Looney for violating the National Motor Vehicle Theft Act. This law, often called the Dyer Act, was passed by Congress in 1919 to make interstate transportation of stolen vehicles a federal crime. The indictment states that in August of 1922, Looney transported across state lines "a certain motor vehicle, to wit: a Hudson Super Six Seven passenger automobile …contrary to the form of the statute…and against the peace and dignity of the United States of America." Warrants for his arrest were sent to federal officers in Santa Fe but these were all returned with a "Not Found" notation. Around this time, there was also a $2,000 reward offer issued for him by the Pinkerton Detective Agency. On December 30, 1922, the Santa Fe *New Mexican* reported Illinois state officials, the FBI, and private detectives were all on his trail.

Looney managed to remain a fugitive for nearly a year but his luck ran out the week of November 30, 1923, when he was arrested at Belen. After he was admitted to the New Mexico State Penitentiary for safekeeping, Looney underwent several days of hearings before a U. S. Commissioner in Santa Fe while Illinois officials attempted to have him extradited to face charges there for the murder of a saloon keeper who had refused "to pay tribute." Looney opposed the extradition, contending he had many enemies because he used his newspaper in Rock Island to expose corrupt judges, bankers, and a "pernicious array of officials who have looted the public treasury." He also told of several attempts on his life and how his son had been killed in one such attack. His arguments apparently convinced the federal commissioner to reject the Illinois request for extradition and held Looney over for trial on the federal Dyer Act charge but I have not found any evidence he was ever tried in federal court.

In late 1925 Looney was finally convicted of murder and conspiracy in Knox County, Illinois and sentenced to fourteen years in Joliet State Prison. He was released in 1934. What became of him after he served his time? Some sources say he moved back to the southwest and died at a tuberculosis sanitarium in El Paso in 1947. Art Daggett, however, wrote that after Looney served his time, he returned to Rio Arriba "a broken man," and died at Gallina shortly after his release.

There is a lot to wonder about John Looney. He was in fact, as my grandmother told us, a fugitive from the law during the time he was in New Mexico. He is also a legendary criminal figure in the city of Rock Island. The city has official "John Looney Legend" bus tours of sites associated with his criminal activities. His local fame and reputation were reflected in the motion picture "The Road to Perdition," in which the character of "John Rooney" portrayed by Paul Newman, was supposedly based on Looney's criminal career. It seems that "el Looney," the "Chicago gangster," is also part of Rio Arriba's colorful history.

A Turquoise Tragedy

Turquoise is the New Mexico State Gem. Chemically, turquoise is described as "hydrous phosphate of aluminum," a mineral that contains small quantities of copper and iron from which the stone derives its blue color. However, this technical description does not do justice to the important role this magnificent stone has played in New Mexico history. For centuries, New Mexico's Indians prized turquoise and mined the gem from various locations. Some of the most ancient of these mines are located in the Cerrillos hills south of Santa Fe. At the center of these is Mount Chalchihuitl, the site of one of the most extensive prehistoric mining operations in North America.

Native Americans from the nearby Pueblos mined these ancient turquoise deposits for centuries. When the Cerrillos region underwent a silver mining boom in the 1800s, prospectors who came across the turquoise deposits caused some to wonder if the blue stones were commercially valuable. Prominent Santa Fe businessmen and investors, including political figures and former governors Lew Wallace and L. Bradford Prince, bought or otherwise schemed to gain control of the most promising claims. Eastern companies such as the American Turquoise Company invested heavily into the exploration and development of these mines. Tiffany's, the famous New York jewelers, reportedly extracted more than two million dollars of turquoise from mines with colorful names such as "Blue Bell," "Morning Star," and "Blue Sky."

These changes meant the Pueblos no longer had free access to the ancient mines that had traditionally supplied this valued resource. However, residents of the nearby pueblos still attempted to enter the mines despite the new owners' best efforts to keep them out. In late 1908, Jonathan Matthews, secretary of the American Turquoise Company (with offices at 52 Wall Street in New York), wrote to Governor George Curry and complained that "the Indians in that vicinity are again trespassing upon our property; stealing stones…"

Matthews included a litany of recent complains he had received from J. P. McNulty, the company' mine superintendent at Cerrillos. McNulty indicated the Indians had been causing him trouble for some time, but recently, he was having problems that were "worse than …ever." He indicated the Indians were persistent, breaking into the Muñiz mine at least twice a week despite the dogs he kept to protect the sites. One night in November 1908, he was even shot at several times, but according to McNulty, "…as God was with me, they missed their mark." He also complained that local officials seemed reluctant to investigate the incidents and take any action. "[We] would respectfully ask that permanent protection be given to our property and to those who reside upon it," concluded Matthews.

When influential economic interests such as these complained, local political officials tended to respond quickly. The specific actions taken by Governor Curry are unknown, but by early 1911, an interesting indictment is found in the Santa Fe County District Court records. On March 10, 1911, a grand jury indicted four Cochiti men, Marcial Quintana, Antonio Trujillo, Cipriano Quintana, and Natividad Quintana. The indictment specifies that on December 18, 1910, the men "did …burglariously (sic) enter the Turquoise Mine known as the Castillian Mine…with intent…to take, steal and carry away the turquoise then being the goods and property of the American Turquoise Company, a corporation…"

Details of the incident and the men's capture are not reflected in the official record. Court records show only that the four were convicted of burglary and on March 10, 1911, they were sentenced to six to nine months in the territorial penitentiary. In those days, each inmate was asked why they had committed the crime for which they were imprisoned and the answer recorded in the convict's record. The response from all four men was the same. They did so, in their words, "to support my family."

The men were paroled in August of that year after serving five months of their sentence. The American Turquoise Company was no doubt pleased with the outcome of these trials, although their position on the matter is not recorded in the official record. Newspaper reports of the trial suggest that the arrest, conviction and sentences imposed on these four men were meant to teach the Indians a lesson. Up to now, reported the *Santa Fe New Mexican*, it had been impossible to "get [the Indians] to understand that the turquoise mines are no longer public property." One cannot help but wonder what lessons these four men and their families learned about American justice and private enterprise.

The Ordeal of Two Lost Heads

The Rio Arriba County courthouse in Tierra Amarilla has been the site of numerous judicial proceedings as well as some well-known and infamous incidents. The colorful history of this courthouse was augmented on August 26, 1982 when workmen conducting routine excavations near the foundation on the east side of the building, unearthed glass jars that contained the disembodied heads of two men. Police and the Office of Medial Investigator were naturally called in to investigate this gruesome find.

Utilizing information provided by various local residents, investigators soon determined the heads were the remains of two men who had been murdered near El Vado in early January 1922. The heads were buried behind the courthouse after they were used as evidence in one of the most sensational trials ever held in Rio Arriba County.

In January 1922 the frozen bodies of Frank Akin and Clay Carpenter were discovered in an arroyo near an abandoned cabin about twelve miles from the then thriving lumber town of El Vado. Investigators determined that Carpenter had been shot in the head and Akin had been struck with a blunt instrument that fractured his skull and apparently killed him instantly. On the same day of the homicides, a man identified as Price Clements was at El Vado, where he sold a number of articles that were later determined to have belonged to the victims. Clements was later apprehended in Matador, Texas.

The scant trial record shows Clements was indicted by a Rio Arriba grand jury on charges of first-degree murder in June 1922. As was the practice of the time, the defendant was arraigned and brought to trial almost immediately after the grand jury returned the indictment. Great excitement prevailed in Tierra Amarilla. The grand jury had also brought an indictment for murder against Francisco Trujillo and Felix Lovato, charged with shooting Canjilón postmaster Tircio de Vargas. Trujillo and Lovato, however, sought and were granted a change of venue to McKinley County due to hard feelings allegedly held against the defendants by many local residents.

The Clements case proved to be one of the most sensational trials in Rio Arriba history. Dr. James Dunham, a Chama physician who practiced medicine in the region for several decades, provided testimony on the injuries inflicted on the murdered victims. His methodology, however, caused quite as stir. Instead of using illustrations or simple descriptions, Dr. Dunham exhumed the long buried victims, severed the heads from their frozen bodies, and presented them at court to illustrate to the jury how the men had been killed. Reports suggest prosecutors did this to refute defense claims as to the nature of the injuries that caused their death. "Severed Heads of Dead Men Before Slayer," declared the headlines in the *Santa Fe New Mexican*. "The heads were a gruesome sight," reported the paper. They were also apparently very effective, as the jury quickly convicted Clements of first-degree murder and sentenced him to death by hanging.

The case, however, was appealed and a new trial allowed. When Clements was retried a year later he was again convicted of first degree murder and sentenced to death by hanging. A final review by the New Mexico Supreme Court in June 1926 looked at several issues. Interestingly, the issue of the gruesome evidence and its undue influence was not addressed by the superior court. It instead considered other elements of the trial testimony and an interesting accusation by the defense that a court officer had tampered with the jury. The Supreme Court, however, affirmed the second verdict and sentence and reset Clements' execution for October 29, 1926.

Clements' date with the hangman, however, was permanently postponed when Governor Arthur T. Hannett commuted his death sentence to life imprisonment. The sensational nature of the trial and lingering issues related to the alleged jury pampering apparently weighted heavily in Governor Hannett's decision. Despite the life sentence, Clements did not spend much time behind bars. On December 23, 1930, Governor Richard C. Dillon further commuted Clements' sentence from life to ten years, noting his "valuable service to the state as a finger print expert." Little more than six months later, Clements was paroled and released from the penitentiary. On the recommendation of the Superintendent, Governor Arthur Seligman granted Clements "a full and complete pardon" on December 21, 1932.

After the trial, the severed heads of Frank Akin and Clay Carpenter were placed in glass jars and apparently displayed at the courthouse for a short period. The macabre exhibits were then buried in shallow graves along the foundation on the east side of the courthouse, where they remained until their accidental discovery in 1982. After examination by the Office of Medical Examiner, the skulls are said to have been reburied in the old cemetery at El Vado State Park, a few miles from the site where they were murdered more than a half century earlier.

El Vado Cemetery where the remains of Frank Akin and Clay Carpenter are said to have been reburied. Robert J. Tórrez Photo.

"Jerked to Jesus"

For a number of years, I have made the point that while a number (but not all) of lynchings in territorial New Mexico utilized trees to carry out their lawless intent, there is no evidence trees were utilized in any of territorial New Mexico's fifty two legal hangings. The title of my book, *Myth of the Hanging Tree*, is based on that premise. Legal executions in territorial New Mexico took place on gallows constructed specifically for the occasion. These ranged from very simple devices, consisting of two upright poles supporting a cross-beam under which a wagon was driven to serve as a mobile platform. Others, such as the scaffold built for the simultaneous hanging of four men in Santa Fe in 1897, were much more complex.

On two occasions, however, a unique device called a "jerk" model was used to carry out legal hangings. The earlier of these was utilized in Las Vegas for the September 12, 1870 execution of Roy Frank (aka Roy French). Well-known Presbyterian missionary Gabino Rendón, tells us in his book, *Hand on My Shoulder*, that he was about twelve when he witnessed the execution of Roy Frank. Rendón recalled the gallows was a crude device:

> On a pole was hinged a cross-bar, longer at one end than the other. At the end of the longer section hung a rope with a noose in the end of it. At the end of the shorter section hung two gunny sacks full of stones. To keep the long bar from flying upward until the proper time, it was held down by a rope attached to a stake driven into the ground.

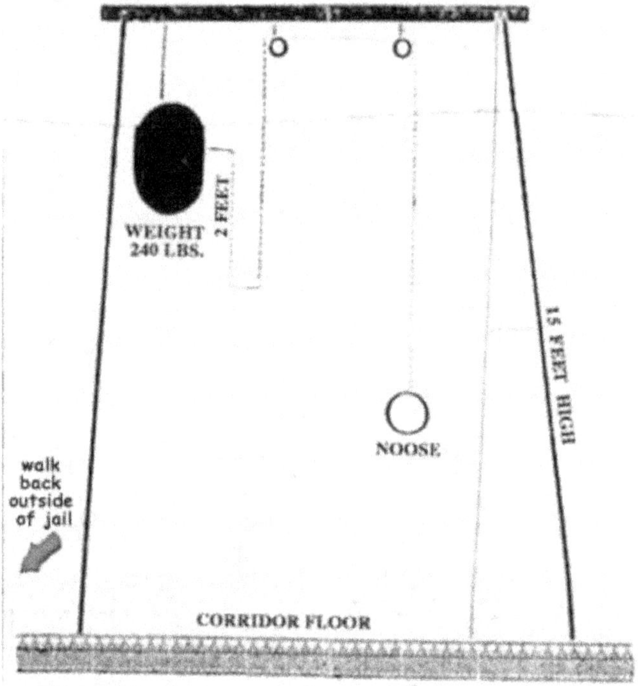

"Sketch of the Machine of Death," McKean County Miner (Smethport, Pennsylvania) December 15, 1893.

San Miguel County Sheriff Juan Romero stood close by, with a deputy at the ready with a sharp hatchet in his hand. Rendon continued:

> A black cap was slipped over the man's eyes. The noose dropped over his head onto his shoulders. Frank Roto held his hatchet ready at the taut rope.
>
> "The Lord have mercy on your soul," said John Annin [a Presbyterian missionary who operated a "free school" in Las Vegas]. The hatchet cut through the rope and the [long] end of the bar flew upward, the noose tightening around the man's neck. I can feel again the stopping of my breath and the horror that went through me.

A version of the jerk model was also used for the execution of Milton Yarberry in Albuquerque on February 9, 1883. The device used to hang Yarberry was described by the *Santa Fe Daily New Mexican* as the latest "model of scientific skill," and supposedly "patterned after a description and cut" that appeared in *Scientific American*. The newspaper indicated that Bernalillo County Sheriff Perfecto Armijo had decided to utilize the "jerk plan" instead of the "old fashioned" gallows because the device was supposed to be "a much more certain and quicker way to produce death." The newspaper's description allows one to visualize how the mechanism worked and why this device was called a "jerk" model:

> There is no trap – nothing but the platform, two uprights and cross beams, as a scaffold. The condemned man stands upon the scaffold, the noose encircling his neck, the rope runs over a pulley when it reaches the crossbeam, leaving two feet of slack between the beam and the noose; thence it runs along the beam to the upright and over another pulley down to six feet from the ground, where it ends with a 400 pound weight. A smaller cord holds the weight until the last moment; then it is cut, the weight falls six feet to the ground, the man is jerked six feet into the air and falls back two feet.

The *Santa Fe Daily New Mexican* and Albuquerque's *The Morning Journal* both seem to agree that the upward jerk broke Yarberry's neck and death was instantaneous. The Albuquerque paper, however, added that Yarberry's head struck the crossbeam of the scaffold as his body was violently jerked upward. This gruesome development may have caused officials to wonder whether Yarberry was killed by the jerking action of the rope or by the impact of his head against the crossbeam. This may explain why the "jerk" device was never again utilized in an execution in New Mexico.

Some published versions of the Milton Yarberry execution have claimed that newspapers reported Yarberry was "Jerked to Jesus." When *Myth of the Hanging Tree* was published in 2010 I had not found this particular phrase used in any of the newspapers that reported Yarberry's execution. Instead I suggested that the phrase may have been adapted from the headline of the event in the *Las Vegas Daily Optic*, whose opening headline of their coverage of the hanging was "Yarberry Yanked." Since then, however, I discovered that the catchy but irreverent "Jerked to Jesus" phrase is actually found in the February 8, 1880, *Optic* report on the triple lynching of Tom Henry (aka Thomas Jefferson House), James West, and John Dorsey on Las Vegas' notorious "hanging windmill." That day the paper praised Henry's calm attitude in the moments before he was "jerked to Jesus." So now we know the phrase is genuine, except that it was apparently not applied to the Milton Yarberry execution.

A Fort Union Mystery

There were two types of justice in the 'wild west.' The first was carried out through due process, in which the individual was afforded a legal trial, convicted by a duly constituted jury, and sentenced by a judge. Too often, however, what passed for justice was meted out by groups or individuals that simply took the law into their own hands. "Judge Lynch Held Court at so-and-so Place Last Night" was a too-common headline in local newspapers that reported these extra-legal events that we call lynchings. Over the years I have documented more than 125 lynchings that occurred at or in the vicinity of more than three dozen communities in New Mexico. There are two dozen or so other reports that I have yet been unable to document properly.

Each of these tragic events has a story behind it, but one of New Mexico's most interesting lynchings is one about which we know very little. We do not know the names of those killed by the lynch mob or even when it happened, although indications are it may have taken place in 1872. The only thing we know for certain is that it took place in the vicinity of Fort Union, just north of Las Vegas.

Fort Union is a fascinating place. Established in 1851 to guard the Santa Fe Trail, it also served as a base of operations against Indian raids and a major supply depot for military posts in New Mexico. When the railroad arrived in New Mexico in 1879, the fort's importance as a supply depot gradually diminished and the post was finally abandoned in 1891. Today, the site is a National Monument administered by the National Park Service. Many volumes have and will continue to be written about the importance of this post in the development of frontier New Mexico.

There were several lynchings in the vicinity of Fort Union, but the one which is the topic of today's story is one that may never have come to our attention except for some excavations done in 1958 by the National Park Service (NPS) near the Fort Union site. In April of that year, an NPS employee accidently unearthed the remains of four adult males buried side by side in a shallow grave. Examination of the remains estimated all four were relatively young men between twenty and thirty years old, and all showed signs of either being shot or bludgeoned to death. The first skeleton had signs of two major wounds - a hole in his sternum and another in his forehead. A .50 caliber bullet and a .36 caliber ball were found among his remains. The excavation report suggests this individual may have been shot in the shoulder from a distance, possibly stabbed or bayoneted in the chest and then shot in the forehead at close range. The second had broken bones suggestive of having been beaten to death; number three had a hole in his cranium and a lead ball was found within, suggesting he was shot at close range, possibly execution –style; number four was apparently clubbed in the head.

Fort Union burials. National Park Service, Fort Union National Monument. Stabalization record, Neg. FOUN 184 S.

Examination of the remains suggests these four men were captured, beaten, shot and hastily buried. But who were they and what did they do to deserve such a brutal death? Who killed them? While we may never find satisfactory answers to these questions, other historical evidence provides some hints of the circumstances surrounding these deaths. Examination of the few surviving pieces of clothing, musket and pistol balls, and other physical evidence led archaeologists to conclude these men were killed sometime between 1863 and 1872. If these dates are correct, it is possible these were the four men reported killed in late July 1872 in a report published in the August 13, 1872 *Daily New Mexican.* The paper carried a brief story of four Loma Parda residents who had been violently killed three weeks earlier because they been "too intimately associated with their neighbor's stock." The newspaper suggests a familiar scenario for that time and place in our history - four men caught stealing cattle or other livestock by citizens who "had more faith in a stout lariat than in stone walls" and therefore decided to take the law into their own hands.

Certainly, the remains of the four men buried near Fort Union show injuries inflicted at close range and in apparent anger. Were these young men hardened rustlers finally caught in the act and punished by men who were normally law-abiding citizens but who were fed-up with having their livestock stolen and livelihood threatened? The archeological report of the remains found in 1958 does not mention any of the men showed signs of having been hanged, so it is possible the 1872 newspaper report referred to some other quadruple lynching; or possibly, it was these four men and the newspaper simply assumed they had been killed by hanging. We will probably never know. The accidental discovery of the rude grave in which these men were hurriedly buried may remain one of the fascinating mysteries of our violent frontier past.

The Ordeal of Ramona Santillanes

In all the years of research I have done about crime and punishment in New Mexico, one of the most tragic, brutal, and yet fascinating elements of our history is the introduction of lynching to New Mexico after the U. S. occupation on 1846. During the Spanish and Mexican periods of our history our ancestors apparently did not take the law into their own hands in this violent extralegal manner.

The first documented lynchings I have found in New Mexico took place in 1850. The last one I have found took place in 1928. During the intervening decades, at least 130 men were lynched under a myriad of circumstances. One interesting element of these findings is that there is no primary evidence a woman was ever lynched in New Mexico.

Marc Simmons, in a story entitled "A Bloodthirsty Family," tells about two men and two women who lived in the mountains of central New Mexico in the 1880s. This family apparently made their living by killing and robbing unsuspecting travelers who had the misfortune of stopping at their cabin to rest and eat. When their bloodthirsty acts were finally uncovered, the men of the house were killed and the two women hanged. However, I have been unable to substantiate the story through available primary evidence. If we one day find more information on this story, these two unnamed women might then be considered the only females lynched in New Mexico.

There is however, primary documentation of one woman who was lynched but managed to survive her ordeal and even attempted to bring her assailants to justice. A fascinating series of documents in the Bernalillo

County District Court records tell us about Ramona Santillanes. Ramona's saga began on April 1, 1884 when a warrant was issued by Justice of the Peace Hernando Armijo of Corrales, a community located north of Albuquerque. The warrant ordered Ramona to appear before Armijo to respond to charges that she was somehow involved with the mysterious disappearance of her husband, Jesús Sandoval. As Santillanes was being escorted to Armijo's house, a group of men (one witness indicated there were at least thirty) led by Román Gutierrez, Seferino Cloret and Louis Alarid, confronted Santillanes and tied up her escort. They took Ramona into the adjoining woods, where Gutierrez placed a rope around her neck and demanded to know where her husband was. Santillanes insisted she knew nothing about his whereabouts but the vigilantes were persistent. In an effort to solicit her confession, they hoisted her by the neck into the air five times. Unable to obtain any information from her by this method, they removed the noose and took her to Justice Armijo's house, where the understandably shaken woman was interrogated about her husband's disappearance and confronted with the general suspicion that she had killed him. She admitted only that her husband had left their home at two o'clock in the morning of February 9 that year and that he did not tell her where he was going. Unsatisfied with her response, Justice Armijo ordered her jailed to wait the next term of the Bernalillo County grand jury.

Santillanes was allowed bail and released until the grand jury convened the following month. In the meantime, she took the offensive and filed her own complaint against Gutierrez and his accomplices. Her complaint noted that Gutierrez, Cloret and Alarid had hanged her by the neck "with force and arms...maliciously and feloniously and with intent to commit the crime of murder."

During the subsequent May 1884 term of Bernalillo County District Court, however, the grand jury failed to prosecute Ramona's assailants. Bernalillo County Criminal case # 471, "Territory of New Mexico –vs- Román Gutierrez, et. al.", charges the three men with assaulting Ramona Santillanes with "intent to kill." The indictment, however, was returned "No true bill." The grand jury also considered an indictment against Ramona (case #475, Territory –vs- Ramona Santillanes), for the murder of her husband, but this was also returned as "no bill found."

Thus ended the story of the only woman *almost* lynched in New Mexico. This is also one of the rare cases in which there was legal action aimed at those who participated in a lynching. The grand jury refused to indict Gutierrez and his accomplices because they obviously found nothing criminal about their actions and may have even felt that local officials had failed to properly investigate the widely held suspicion that Ramona Santillanes had killed her husband. They also apparently did not find any evidence that she actually had anything to do with his disappearance. Maybe Jesús subsequently showed up at their home with some lame explanation of where he had been. Maybe he was dead, a victim of some unknown assailant. On the other hand, maybe Ramona got away with something. *¡Quien sabe!* Thus are the unexplained mysteries of our fascinating past.

INDEX

G

H

I

J

K

N

O

P

Q

R

S

CPSIA information can be obtained
at www.ICGtesting.com
Printed in the USA
BVHW071250240719
554234BV00010B/1028/P

9 781943 681181